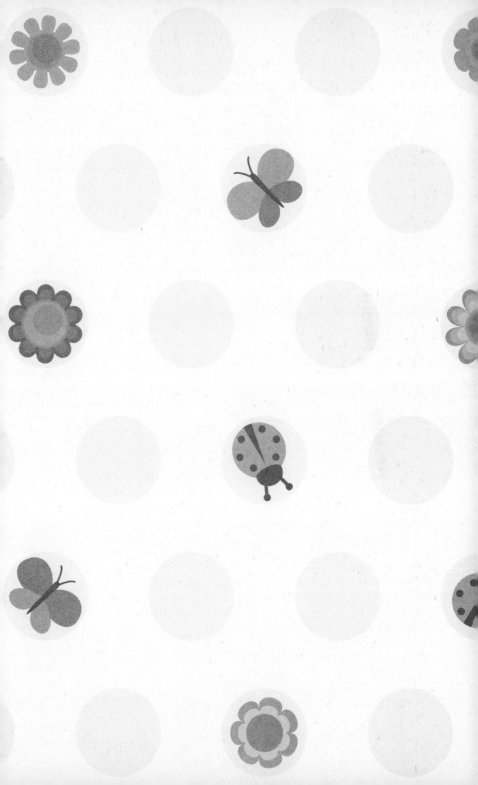

promises for God's Princesses

Katrina Cassel

Tyndale House Publishers, Inc.
Carol Stream, Illinois

Visit www.cool2read.com.

TYNDALE and Tyndale's quill logo are registered trademarks of Tyndale House Publishers, Inc.

Promises for God's Princesses

Designed by Jacqueline L. Nuñez

Edited by Erin Gwynne

For manufacturing information regarding this product, please call 1-800-323-9400.

Library of Congress Cataloging-in-Publication Data

Cassel, Katrina L., date.
  Promises for God's princesses / Katrina Cassel.
    pages cm
    ISBN 978-1-4143-9660-6 (hc)
  1. Girls—Religious life—Juvenile literature.   2. Bible—Devotional use—Juvenile literature.   I. Title.
    BV4551.3.C38 2014
    248.8'2—dc23   2014014349

Printed in the United States of America

20   19   18   17   16   15   14
 7   6   5   4   3   2   1

To my princesses:
Jessica, Jasmine, and Kayla

Contents

x

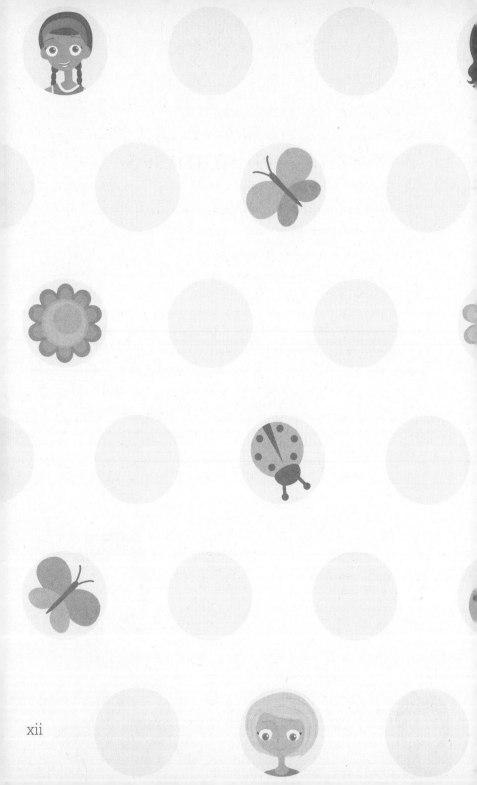

1

Princess Promises

*Because of [God's] glory and excellence, he has
given us great and precious promises.*

2 PETER 1:4

A lot of people like watching royal families. They
look for news about kings, queens, princes, and
princesses. They buy special editions of magazines or
collectors' books devoted to special events like royal
weddings and royal births. When Prince William of
Great Britain married Kate Middleton, many Americans
got up in the early hours of the morning to watch
the wedding because of time-zone differences. When
William and Kate's baby was due to be born, people
around the world eagerly awaited news of the royal
baby's birth.

Did you know you are royalty? No, you weren't
born into a royal family, and your father or mother
probably doesn't sit on a throne and wear a crown. You
aren't on television waving to the crowds or presid-
ing over a royal event. But if you have confessed your
sins and decided to live for God, you are a daughter
of the heavenly King, and that makes you one of his
own princesses.

Today's verse says your heavenly King has many special promises and words of instruction for you. Some of these instructions will help you grow to be more like Jesus as you daily seek to follow God (see Philippians 2:2-4). The promises you'll read can help you face whatever problems or joys each day may bring. If you're discouraged, they give you new hope (see John 16:33). If you're tired, they give you strength (see Isaiah 40:31). If you're afraid, they give you courage (see Deuteronomy 31:6).

God's promises guide you in the right direction and remind you of who you are in him. As you read through this book, you will encounter many promises God has given you, as well as verses with instructions for your life. Take time to read them, think about them, and understand how they can help you.

Write down at least one Bible verse with a promise or instruction God has given you. How does it apply to your life today? If you can't think of any, look up the verses mentioned above and choose one that speaks to you. Or you can use the concordance in the back of your Bible or an online concordance to locate verses. Just look for a key word such as *courage*, *peace*, or *strength*, and see what verses are listed. These are God's promises just for you!

For the Lord is good his Steadfast love endures forever Psalms: 100: 5 (Part A)

2

A Child of God

*To all who believed [Jesus] and accepted him,
he gave the right to become children of God.*

JOHN 1:12

You and every other baby born have both a father
and a mother. Who your parents are determines
what you look like, what talents you have, and more.
You resemble your parents in many ways. Your voice
may sound similar to your mother's, and your hair
and eyes may be the same color as hers. Or you may
be tall like your dad and share his musical ability.

Did you know that you also resemble God? He
created you in his image. That doesn't mean he
shares your red hair and freckles or brown skin and
chocolate eyes. He's not left or right handed. But even
though you don't look like him physically, you are like
him in other ways. You have a spiritual nature. You
can think and choose. You can create. You can act in
godly ways. You can tell right from wrong.

God's first children, Adam and Eve, were also
made in his image, but they disobeyed his rules. Ever
since then every person is born with a sinful nature.
It's easier for us to choose to do wrong. God knew

that would happen, and he had a plan ready. He sent his Son, Jesus, to live a sinless life here on earth and then die on the cross to pay the penalty for sin. But that's not all. Jesus came back to life and defeated sin and death.

Because of what Jesus did, you can have a place in God's family. If you believe that Jesus died for you and ask him to take away the bad things in your heart, you become a child of God. As you choose to follow him daily, you look more and more like him. Each morning, ask God to show you what he wants you to do for him that day. He'll show you who needs a kind word or a helping hand. He will lead you in making right choices and choosing to overcome the temptation to do wrong. He'll give you the desire to please him. And he will help you live victoriously as a daughter of God and child of the King.

List ways that you are like your family. Do you look like your mom? Do you share your dad's talents? Do you have the same interests as your siblings? The same favorite foods? Next, list ways you are like your heavenly Father. What characteristics do you share with him? See Galatians 5:22-23 if you need some ideas.

3
Puzzle Pieces

"I know the plans I have for you," says the Lord.
"They are plans for good and not for disaster,
to give you a future and a hope."

Jeremiah 29:11

Have you ever done a jigsaw puzzle? Most of the pieces are just bits of color. Is that blue piece a bit of sky or water? Is the green piece part of the grass or a leaf? The red looks like part of the barn, or maybe it's part of the wagon. You may not know what each piece is, but when you put all the pieces together, they form a picture.

Your life may seem like that puzzle to you. One day the girl who rides the bus with you acts like she's your friend, but the next day she makes fun of you. You practice for weeks for a lead role in the musical, but you are offered only a part in the chorus. You pray for your grandmother who is very sick, but she dies anyway. Your best friend moves away because of her dad's job, and you don't think you'll find another friend like her. Sometimes life doesn't make sense. That's because each of those events is just one puzzle piece, not the whole picture.

Not seeing the whole picture can make the individual events of your life seem confusing. Good things happen. Bad things happen. Some days you just don't know what to expect. That's because you're only seeing that small piece of your life. Who knows where today's events may lead down the road?

God does! He sees the whole picture at once. He created a special plan just for you. And he uses things that don't always make sense to you, both good and bad, to work out his plan. He knows what he wants you to accomplish for him, and he's given you everything you need to succeed. So when life doesn't make sense to you, trust that the things happening today—the individual puzzle pieces—are part of the bigger picture: God's special plan for you.

Put a jigsaw puzzle together with a friend or family member. (If you don't have a puzzle, you can usually buy one at a dollar store or even make one by cutting a magazine picture into pieces.) Talk about how God's plan is like that puzzle.

4
On Wings of Eagles

Those who trust in the LORD will find new strength.
They will soar high on wings like eagles. They will run
and not grow weary. They will walk and not faint.

ISAIAH 40:31

The founders of the United States of America
wanted a bird that would represent the country.
In 1782 they chose the bald eagle as the national bird,
although some, like Benjamin Franklin, preferred the
turkey. The bald eagle is not really bald, but it has
short white feathers on its head. Experts believe that
"bald" might be from the Old English word *balde*, which
means "white." With wide wings, this bird of prey soars
high in the sky and symbolizes courage, majesty, and
freedom. The eagle appears on the Great Seal of the
United States and on many coins.

It's no wonder that Isaiah chose to use the eagle
as an illustration of what happens when you put
your trust in the Lord. With God, you can soar high
like the eagle. Sometimes life is tough, and you might
not feel as if you're soaring. You might feel more like
you're crawling! It's easy to get discouraged or to feel
like giving up. That's normal. But God is mighty and

powerful, and he's able to handle all your problems. He doesn't want you to be held back by discouragement, failure, sadness, or fear. He wants to give you strength and courage to meet your challenges. Whether you're facing a difficult school assignment, dealing with relationship problems, or struggling to understand what it means to be a Christian, God wants you to turn to him. Ask for guidance, and be sensitive to what he tells you when he speaks to your heart—through prayer, through a parent's advice, or through a pastor's sermon.

When you trust God and follow his leading, you'll soar above life's difficulties just as an eagle soars high above land. Think about the eagle today, and decide that you will let God help you rise on wings like eagles as you listen to him and seek to do the things he wants you to do.

Find three interesting facts about eagles using the Internet, a book, or an encyclopedia. Why do you think Isaiah used the example of an eagle and not a different bird? How does the eagle symbolize your relationship with God?

5
No One's Perfect

If we confess our sins to [God], he is faithful and just to
forgive us our sins and to cleanse us from all wickedness.

1 JOHN 1:9

You may have heard someone say, "No one's perfect," after making a mistake. Perhaps your friend forgot she was going to call you or that she promised to let you use her math book. Or maybe your sister borrowed something of yours and lost it. Your friend or sister may say, "No one's perfect," in hopes that you'll overlook what she did. Her response may or may not work, but it is true that no one's perfect. Everyone, even God's special princesses, messes up at times.

Sometimes when you mess up, it's a real mistake. You may have accidentally knocked over your glass of milk. Or maybe you forgot to finish your homework assignment. Other times you may do something that breaks one of God's rules for you. Maybe something made you angry, and you lashed out at your mom or dad. Or maybe you saw that a classmate got the very outfit you wanted but couldn't get because your mom said it was too expensive. Jealousy took over, and you

said something unkind to cover your feelings. Perhaps you panicked when you couldn't remember an answer on the history test, and you peeked at your classmate's uncovered answers. All these things are wrong and make you feel unclean, or guilty, on the inside.

The good news is that you don't have to live with that bad feeling. No matter what you've done, you can tell God about it. He's promised to forgive you. That forgiveness takes away the guilt in your heart and replaces it with peace. God gives you joy in place of guilt. So don't let bad feelings build up. Talk to God about your mistakes, and accept his forgiveness.

If you aren't sure your heart is clean, pray these words that David prayed: "Search me, O God, and know my heart; test me and know my anxious thoughts. Point out anything in me that offends you, and lead me along the path of everlasting life" (Psalm 139:23-24).

6
Powerful Love

*No power in the sky above or in the earth below—
indeed, nothing in all creation will ever be
able to separate us from the love of God that
is revealed in Christ Jesus our Lord.*

ROMANS 8:39

Have you ever read a story in the newspaper or heard one on TV about a parent who did something extraordinary to save a child who was in danger, such as lifting a car to free a trapped child or fighting a wild animal to rescue a son or daughter? That's how strong a parent's love is. This love causes moms and dads to desire the best for their children and to protect them at all cost. Now think about the fact that as much as a parent loves a child and wants to protect him or her, your heavenly Father loves you more. His love is even stronger and more powerful than a parent's love.

God's love is not only strong but also unconditional. That means he loves you no matter what you do. He loves you when you say something nice to a brother or sister, and he loves you when you say something mean. God's love for you doesn't depend on

what you do. God loves you because of who he is. First John 4:10 says, "This is real love—not that we loved God, but that he loved us and sent his Son as a sacrifice to take away our sins." God loved us so much that before we were even born, he sent his Son to die on the cross for our sins. His love for you is eternal. His kind of love never goes away; it never ends. God's love is with you whether you're celebrating or crying. It's with you when you're victorious or when you're being tempted. It's with you during your happiest times and during your toughest tests. God's love is with you 24-7.

You can live confidently today because God's love will never let you go.

Read 1 John 4. List the things it says about love. How can you apply them to your life today?

I† says that God loved us first and that is why we love.
This applys to my life because
I need love because I feel unloved a lot during quarentine

7
Heavenly Rooms

There is more than enough room in my Father's home. If this were not so, would I have told you that I am going to prepare a place for you? When everything is ready, I will come and get you, so that you will always be with me where I am.

JOHN 14:2-3

Picture your dream bedroom. What paint color would be on the walls? Would you decorate it with posters? Or pictures of your best friends? Would your room have a lamp or a ceiling fan with an overhead light? A blanket with characters from your favorite movie or a plain one in your favorite color? What furniture would it have? Bunk beds? A desk for you to write at? Your dream room might have a sports theme or perhaps a movie theme or just all your favorite colors.

Do you know that God is preparing a special room for you?

No one knows exactly what heaven will be like, but the Bible describes a new heaven and a new earth where the walls of the city will be covered with precious stones like sapphires and emeralds. The gates

of the city will be made of pearl, and the streets will be covered by pure gold.

What kind of room will you have in heaven? God didn't share all the details in the Bible. But God is a creative God. Just look at all the different things in nature—clouds, trees, sky, grass, and animals. We can guess that he'll use that same creativity in designing our heavenly homes. And it may be that he is specially designing each room for the person who will live there. Pictures often show heaven as having elaborate mansions of gold, but we don't know if that's what heaven will look like. One thing is for sure, though—whatever kind of room he's preparing for you, it will be just perfect.

Although you don't know what your eternal home will look like, you can be sure that God is creating a very special place for you. Read Revelation 21, and list the things it says about your heavenly home.

- There will be no death or moorning or pain.
- There is rare jewls like jasper a clear a crystal.
- A great high wall w/ 12 gates 12 angels at the gates and on the gates 12 tribe names are written
- wall buit of jasper
- pure gold
- Every kind of jewl
- Glory of god gives all right
- No night

8
Peace for God's Princesses

[Jesus said,] "I am leaving you with a gift—peace of mind and heart. And the peace I give is a gift the world cannot give. So don't be troubled or afraid."

JOHN 14:27

Think of all the gifts you've ever been given. Does one stand out as your favorite? Did you receive a gift that was more special than the others? You may have gotten something you'd wanted for a long time. Or maybe you got something you really needed. Jesus gave his disciples a gift he knew they'd need, and it was something only he could give them. That gift was peace.

When Jesus told his disciples they'd have peace, he didn't mean they wouldn't face any hard times or trouble. He knew they would. The peace he offered them was a knowledge in their minds and a feeling in their hearts no matter what was going on around them. Jesus knew his disciples would face hard times. They would suffer for preaching about him. Some would even be killed for their faith. But that didn't change their confidence in God and their confidence that God would use everything that happened to spread his good news.

As one of God's princesses, you can have that same peace. It's the peace that allows you to walk with your head held high—because you belong to your heavenly King—no matter what is happening around you. If someone is teasing you, peace reminds you that God loves you. If you're worried about tomorrow's math test, peace lets you know that God is always with you.

So how can you receive this special gift? Peace comes from having a relationship with Jesus. If you have asked Jesus to forgive your sins and you've made a decision to live for him, you can experience his peace.

Write today's verse on a card or piece of paper and put it where you can see it often (like your bathroom mirror or above the light switch in your room). Ask God to give you his peace to get you through any tough times you are facing this week.

9
Ordinary People

Each time [God] said, "My grace is all you need.
My power works best in weakness." So now I
am glad to boast about my weaknesses, so that
the power of Christ can work through me.

2 CORINTHIANS 12:9

There are a lot of pageants, competitions, and award ceremonies people take part in. These can be as simple as crowning a queen at the local county fair or holding a citywide math, spelling, or music competition. Or they can be as grand as the Miss America Pageant, award shows for best movie or music of the year, or the Super Bowl. At these big events, people compete on television, and winners receive beautiful tiaras or huge trophies for their accomplishments.

Although the winners at big events receive a lot of honor and recognition, God doesn't single these people out to do his work. He doesn't choose only the beautiful or handsome people. He doesn't search for the smartest or richest or most athletic ones. That doesn't mean he won't use those people, but he doesn't choose people based on what they look like or on what they can do. When God chooses, he looks for people who

are willing. That means they want to serve him. Oftentimes these are ordinary people whom others may easily overlook.

Think about your favorite Bible characters. Most were ordinary people before God called them. Andrew, Peter, James, and John were fishermen. Matthew was a tax collector. Noah and Elisha were farmers. Moses, David, and Amos were shepherds. Yet God used them. It didn't matter whether they were rich or poor, educated or uneducated. They were all willing, and God used them.

It doesn't matter if you're the best in your class at math or struggle with your homework, if you play volleyball or can't get your serve over the net. It doesn't matter if you make the honor roll or earn straight Cs. God has something special for you to do for him. And he is asking you to be willing.

Can you list 10 Bible characters and what their jobs were? Ask your friends or family to help you add names to the list. Why do you think God often uses ordinary people rather than the strongest, smartest, and best looking?

10

The Way Out

The temptations in your life are no different from what others experience. And God is faithful. He will not allow the temptation to be more than you can stand. When you are tempted, he will show you a way out so that you can endure.

1 CORINTHIANS 10:13

Corn mazes are popular destinations in the fall. These mazes are paths that are cut through cornfields. If you saw them from above, they would sometimes have fun designs or shapes, and they might look like the mazes printed in a puzzle book. For a corn maze, you enter the maze and have to find the right path out. Sometimes that can be tricky or confusing. You can make wrong turns and hit dead ends or walk in circles without knowing it. The same is true when you face temptation. It may be tricky or confusing to find a way out of the temptation and avoid sinning. Thankfully, you have God to guide you through a temptation maze.

God knows his princesses face temptations every day. People have faced temptations since the beginning of the world. A serpent tempted Adam and Eve

to disobey and break God's rule for them to not eat the forbidden fruit. Your temptation may be to break God's rules by looking at things on the Internet that don't honor him. Or disobeying your mom or dad by texting a friend when you are supposed to be doing homework.

Because your heavenly King doesn't want you to give in to the urge to do wrong, he's given you escape routes. You might need to leave a friend's house and go home if she wants to watch a movie you know you shouldn't watch. Or maybe you'll have to find someone different to sit with at lunch if your friends are making fun of other kids in the cafeteria. You might need to turn off the TV or computer if something that dishonors God flashes across the screen. There is always an escape, a way to avoid giving in to temptation, but you have to be willing to take that way out even though it might not always be easy.

When you are tempted, ask God to show you the way out of the temptation maze . . . and get out of there.

Make a list of five things you can do when you are tempted. Include people you might be able to talk to and things you can do to avoid sinning.

11

It's All Good

*We know that God causes everything to work
together for the good of those who love God and
are called according to his purpose for them.*

ROMANS 8:28

It's fun to watch the news when there are stories of
heroic deeds or happy events. But when there are
tornadoes, wars, fires, or car accidents, it's easier to
change the channel. No one wants to hear the bad
news. Good things happen. Bad things happen. But
don't let that discourage you. God can use both the
good and bad things that happen in your life today.

This is absolutely true all the time. God can use
the things we consider bad, as well as the good things,
in order to accomplish his plans. Just look at Joseph
from the Bible (see Genesis 37). His brothers were
jealous of him, so they sold him into slavery. Poor
Joseph probably thought that was the worst thing that
could ever happen to him. He must have felt aban-
doned and wondered why God allowed it.

Yet later Joseph was able to see how God had used
this dark point in his life to help him provide food for
the Egyptian people during a severe famine. While

Joseph was in Egypt, the pharaoh had a confusing dream about seven fat cows and seven skinny cows. Then the pharaoh had another dream about stalks of grain. God showed Joseph that both dreams meant a famine was coming. There would be no rain, so no crops would grow. That meant there would be no food to eat.

Because Joseph was in Egypt, he was able to warn the pharaoh of the coming famine. That meant the pharaoh was able to prepare for the famine ahead of time so there would be grain to feed the people during the years when nothing would grow. People, including Joseph's brothers, also came from other countries for food.

When Joseph was reunited with his brothers many years after they had sold him, Joseph told them, "You intended to harm me, but God intended it all for good. He brought me to this position so I could save the lives of many people" (Genesis 50:20).

God can use both the good and bad events of your life to carry out his plan. He did it for Joseph, and he'll do it for you, too.

How have you seen God bring something good out of a bad situation? Tell someone about that time and how it affected your faith in God.

12

Following the Shepherd

[Jesus said,] "My sheep listen to my voice; I know them, and they follow me. . . . My Father has given them to me, and he is more powerful than anyone else. No one can snatch them from the Father's hand."

JOHN 10:27, 29

Sheep are followers. It's their nature. If one sheep wanders off, the others are right behind it. They like to be in flocks and will band together for protection, because it's harder to attack a sheep in a group than one who is alone. In times past, some shepherds would bring their flocks together in a pen at night, to be guarded by a gatekeeper. In the morning, the shepherds would return and call out to their sheep. The sheep would recognize their shepherd's voice and follow him.

Have you ever been in a room and heard your close friend talking to someone outside the room? You recognized her voice right away and may have gone to join her. Or maybe you were outside with friends when your dad called your name. You went home right away because you recognized his voice. It's that same way with Jesus and his sheep—that's you!

Jesus is your shepherd, and he wants to lead you in the safest and best way. He knows what's ahead, so he's able to take you safely through it. Just as a shepherd may lead his sheep away from a rocky ledge or a dangerous animal, Jesus will lead you through tough times, temptations, and tests.

Psalm 23 says that Jesus, the Good Shepherd, supplies all your needs. He leads you on the right paths in even the darkest of times. He has abundant blessings for you when you follow him.

As you hear your shepherd's voice, you can follow him and trust that he will always be with you, always looking out for you and always choosing the right path for you.

Read Psalm 23. Make a list of all the things the Good Shepherd does for his sheep. Look at this list to remember what God has promised to do for you.

13
Growing Fruit

*[Jesus said,] "Remain in me, and I will remain
in you. For a branch cannot produce fruit if
it is severed from the vine, and you cannot
be fruitful unless you remain in me."*

JOHN 15:4

Many people like to grow fruit trees in their back-
yards. Depending on the part of the country you
live in, you might see peaches, pears, cherries, apples,
or oranges on these backyard trees. There's nothing
like being able to walk outside and eat sweet cherries
from your own tree in the spring or crisp apples in the
fall. When there's an abundant crop, the fruit can be
put in the freezer or canned in jars for later.

The trees need care in order to produce their fruit.
They need direct sunlight and water. Some trees need
to have a cold season in order to grow, while others
thrive best in hot climates. All of them need good soil.

Sometimes a tree doesn't produce fruit, or the
fruit rots, but you can be like the trees whose branches
are heavy with good fruit. When you belong to Jesus,
he wants you to abide in him. That means you have
a close personal relationship with him. You read your

Bible, think hard about what you're reading, and let those words change you from the inside out. Just as the sun, rain, and good soil give the trees what they need to produce fruit, Jesus gives you all you need to produce spiritual fruit.

What is spiritual fruit? It isn't the kind you find in an orchard or in the supermarket. It's the characteristics God's Spirit develops in you as you allow him to work in your life. He nudges your conscience about the stuff that doesn't belong—like jealousy, anger, gossip, and unkind thoughts about others. And he helps you make choices that make you more like Jesus.

When that happens, your life will blossom with love, joy, peace, patience, kindness, goodness, faithfulness, gentleness, and self-control (see Galatians 5:22-23). These are called the fruit of the Spirit, and others will see these in your life when you are abiding in Christ.

The fruit of the Spirit are listed above, or you can read them for yourself in Galatians 5:22-23. Can you see these characteristics in your own life? If not, ask God to help you be more like Jesus so that his fruit will fill your life.

14
Chosen for a Purpose

[The Lord said,] "I knew you before I formed you in your mother's womb. Before you were born I set you apart and appointed you as my prophet to the nations."

JEREMIAH 1:5

Picture this scene: You walk into the gym and see that your class is going to be divided into teams for games. Two of your classmates are appointed captains and start to choose their teams from all of the students. If you're athletic or popular, you're probably going to be chosen first. But what if you have a reputation for always missing the basket? Or being the first one out when playing dodgeball? Or what if you're just not popular? You may be picked last, and that's not a good feeling. Especially if your teammates groan when you join them.

The good news is that God doesn't make choices based on your popularity or how smart you are or how athletic you are. He chose you because he wanted to. The even better news is that because you are someone God chose, he already had a plan in mind for you before you were born. You may not know what that plan is yet, and that's okay. You have a lifetime to figure it out. It'll be an adventure as you follow God each day. So instead of getting discouraged in the tough times or in the girl drama that takes place, view each thing that happens to you as another stepping-stone toward God's plans for you. Each day gives you an opportunity to learn and grow as God's princess.

Today's verse says God chose Jeremiah to be a prophet before Jeremiah was even born. God used each thing that happened in Jeremiah's life to prepare him to take God's message to the people.

You can put your own name in Jeremiah 1:5, knowing that God has set you apart to work for him and that he'll help you find what your special job is as you follow him daily. So write out Jeremiah 1:5 and put your name as the first word. Ask God to reveal to you the rest of the verse a day at a time. It should look like this: "_____ (your name), I knew you before I formed you in your mother's womb. Before you were born I set you apart and appointed you as _____."

Your answer might look like one of these:

> a helper for your parents
> a friend to someone who is lonely
> a bright light among the kids in your neighborhood

15
Unfinished

*God, who began the good work within you, will
continue his work until it is finally finished
on the day when Christ Jesus returns.*

PHILIPPIANS 1:6

Sculptors are amazing artists. Some sculpt with clay or sand. Others sculpt with stone. When working with stone, the sculptor starts with a large block of natural stone. He or she may use an electric saw with a masonry blade to make grooves and then use a heavy chisel to remove the larger parts of the stone that aren't needed for the finished project. Or the sculptor may use a smaller chisel to carefully remove a little bit of stone at a time. Trying to take off too much stone at a time could cause damage.

After the rough shape of the sculpture has emerged, a series of different chisels are used. Through the sculptor's careful and controlled efforts, the sculpture starts taking shape. Rough edges are contoured. A file helps smooth things out.

Then comes the sanding. The sculptor starts with a coarse sandpaper and advances to a finer one as the sculpture becomes smoother and smoother, and

the paper and stone may need to be rinsed during the sanding process. It requires care to sand the sculpture, especially the hard-to-reach places, without damaging the piece. The finished product, dust free and dry, might have sculpting rouge or wax applied.

What does this have to do with you, one of God's princesses? God is in the process of shaping and polishing you to make you the person he wants you to be. Like the sculptor, God knows what the finished product—you—should look like. He may have to chisel off rough edges of anger, jealousy, or impatience to help you get to that place.

Unlike a stone statue that can be finished in months or years, God's work of making you all he wants you to be is a lifelong process. He wants you to continue to grow and be polished in order to become like Jesus.

God does this work in you, but you can also do things to help yourself grow in your Christian life. These may include reading your Bible, praying, telling others about your faith, attending church and youth group, helping others, and taking part in ministry projects. All of these, done out of love for Jesus, will help you become who God wants you to be.

What things do you think God wants to chisel out of your life? What one thing can you do today to help you grow in your faith? Write it down, and at the end of the day record how it went.

16

Do Your Best

Work willingly at whatever you do, as though you were working for the Lord rather than for people.
COLOSSIANS 3:23

One school has the motto "Do your best, and the rest will take care of itself." While that may not be entirely true, it's used to motivate the students in their schoolwork and to build pride in their school.

The apostle Paul takes the do-your-best idea one step further and tells his readers to do everything as though they were doing it for the Lord. That's an even higher motivation than doing your best to show school pride. It's doing your best because you are a princess of the heavenly King and you want to please him.

You may be wondering how you can do your best at things you're not very good at. What if you're better at playing a board game with a friend than running a lap in PE class? What if you get an A on your art project and a C on your math assignment? It's simply easier for you to do your best at something you're good at. Or what if you're asked to do something you don't enjoy? If you know that you don't like doing a certain job, activity, or assignment, you're not likely to give it your all.

While that may be true, God wants you to do your best, whether the task is easy or hard for you. He wants your all, whether you like what you are doing or not. If you find that hard to do, remind yourself that your motivation is to please Jesus by the job you do, whether or not you enjoy it and whether or not you're good at it. So next time your teacher gives an extra-long reading or math assignment, or your mom asks you to sweep out the garage, tackle it cheerfully, and know that you're doing it for God.

Think of one thing that is hard for you to do or something that you don't enjoy doing. Ask God to help you do your best for him. You may want to memorize today's verse as a reminder.

17

Think about It

Fix your thoughts on what is true, and honorable, and right, and pure, and lovely, and admirable. Think about things that are excellent and worthy of praise.

PHILIPPIANS 4:8

Your mind is amazing. It can figure out puzzles. It can tell your heart to keep beating. It can remember fun memories from when you were younger. If someone says, "rainbow," a picture of a colorful arch comes to mind. If someone says, "storm," you might imagine a dark sky with rain pelting down or perhaps a sky filled with lightning. Different words trigger different thoughts in your mind, some good and some not.

Because your mind is able to reason, think, and remember, it's powerful. What's in your mind controls your actions, attitudes, and feelings. As God's princess, you want to fill your mind with good things.

It's so important for you to do this that God gave you a list of the types of things he wants you to think about. Those are things that are true, honorable, right, pure, lovely, and admirable. You should think about things that are excellent and worthy of praise.

That's easier said than done. When you get in an argument with your brother or the kid who is supposed to share the bus seat with you, you probably don't think lovely and admirable things. And when your coach makes you run extra laps because a few of your teammates were messing around, your first thoughts may not be honorable or worthy of praise. It's easy to think of mean remarks you'd like to say out loud or to think angry thoughts about the people who caused the problem.

It may take practice to replace those angry or unkind thoughts with those that are pure and lovely, but it's important, because what's in your mind will affect your actions. And your actions tell others what kind of person you are inside. So when your thoughts aren't about things that are true, honorable, right, pure, lovely, and admirable, ask God to help you. When you have good thoughts, you become more like Jesus.

Write the list from Philippians 4:8 on a note card, and put it in your locker at school or on your desk or table if you're homeschooled. Read it often, and practice what it says so that thinking those kinds of thoughts will start feeling more natural.

18

What God Wants

*O people, the LORD has told you what is good, and
this is what he requires of you: to do what is right,
to love mercy, and to walk humbly with your God.*

MICAH 6:8

When you're older, you may want to get a job. You'll probably search the classified ads either in the newspaper or online. The ads will tell you things like what the job is, how much it pays, and how many hours a week you'll work. It may have requirements, too. You may need to be over 18 years old and have a driver's license. You might have to have some experience doing a similar job. You may need certain training or a college education. The employer knows that when an employee meets the requirements, the employee will be able to do the job well.

A verse in Micah gives God's requirements for his people. He wants them to do what is right, to love mercy, and to walk humbly with him. These aren't new instructions. Back in the time of Moses and Joshua, God said, "Now, Israel, what does the LORD your God require of you? He requires only that you fear the LORD your God, and live in a way that pleases him,

and love him and serve him with all your heart and soul" (Deuteronomy 10:12).

How his people lived was always important to God. He wanted them to follow his laws, put him first, and treat one another fairly. Even though you don't live in Old Testament times, God wants his princesses to do these same things today. If you love God with all of your heart, try to put him first in all you do, and live in a way that honors him, he will be pleased.

These verses can be your guide as you complete your schoolwork, do your chores, interact with friends and family members, attend church, and take part in sports activities or music lessons.

List the things Micah 6:8 or Deuteronomy 10:12 says God requires. Think of one way each of those things will impact your daily life. Example: "Serve him with all your heart and soul." I can serve God by cheerfully helping my mom prepare dinner.

19
True Love

Love is patient and kind. Love is not jealous or boastful or proud or rude. It does not demand its own way. It is not irritable, and it keeps no record of being wronged. It does not rejoice about injustice but rejoices whenever the truth wins out. Love never gives up, never loses faith, is always hopeful, and endures through every circumstance.

1 CORINTHIANS 13:4-7

People talk about different kinds of love. There's the love of a parent for a child, the love between two best friends, the love a boy has for a girl, the love between a married couple, or the love a pet owner has for a pet. People also say they love a favorite food, a book, a movie or song, a certain piece of clothing, or a vacation spot.

But do they really love those things? People use the word *love* when they actually mean "like," "enjoy," "prefer," or "care about" something. God talks about true love in 1 Corinthians 13, a chapter of the Bible that is often called the "love chapter." In 1 Corinthians 13, God gives us the qualities of true love: love is patient, kind, not jealous, not boastful,

not proud, not rude, doesn't demand its own way, is not irritable, and doesn't keep track of being wronged.

If you want to know if you really love someone, think about the list from the love chapter. Do you mentally keep track of all the times someone has hurt your feelings? Do you always want to do only *your* favorite activities when you're planning something with your friends? Do you ever get jealous of what someone else has? Are you patient with others?

You can recognize true love, God's kind of love, by looking for the things listed in 1 Corinthians 13.

Look up 1 Corinthians 13 in your Bible. Some of the verses are already listed above. Make a list of the things each verse says about love. How important did the apostle Paul, the man who wrote this chapter, feel love was? How well do you do at loving others based on the signs of real love?

20

Living Water

*Jesus replied, "Anyone who drinks this water will soon
become thirsty again. But those who drink the water
I give will never be thirsty again. It becomes a fresh,
bubbling spring within them, giving them eternal life."*

John 4:13-14

The sixteenth-century Spanish explorer Juan Ponce
de León's name is most often linked to his search
for the Fountain of Youth. According to legend, Juan
searched in what is now Florida for a spring whose
water would restore youth or allow those who drank
it to live forever. Although his search for the Fountain
of Youth is now considered to be just a made-up story,
people still visit Ponce de León's Fountain of Youth
Archaeological Park in St. Augustine, Florida. The idea
of water that can restore youth or allow people to live
forever is appealing.

There may not be a spring in Florida that offers
eternal youth, but there is water that gives eternal
spiritual life. This water, however, is not physical water
at all.

One day Jesus was traveling when he came upon
a woman drawing water from a well. He told her she

would drink that water and be thirsty again later, but if she took the water he offered, she'd never be thirsty again. The woman thought he meant real water that would quench her physical thirst, but Jesus was speaking of water that would quench her spiritual thirst and give her eternal life. He told her many things about her life he couldn't have known, and she realized he was truly the Messiah. She went to her village and brought people back to hear him for themselves. Many people believed in Jesus that day.

Although there is no physical water that can restore youth or give you a long life, Jesus has a better offer—eternal life to those who believe in him.

Find John 4:1-42 in your Bible, and read the story of the woman at the well for yourself. The woman sharing what Jesus did caused many other people to go see Jesus themselves. How can you share the good news of Jesus today?

21

24-7

He will not let you stumble; the one who watches over you will not slumber. Indeed, he who watches over Israel never slumbers or sleeps.

PSALM 121:3-4

You probably go to bed early on school nights so that you get at least eight hours of sleep. You need that amount of sleep in order to do your school-work well. But not all living creatures sleep that amount of time. A brown bat sleeps around 20 hours a day, but a giraffe may sleep as little as 2 hours a day. How much sleep animals and people need may vary by how active they are. A dog that is an only pet may sleep many more hours than a dog that plays with other dogs or works on a farm or ranch. An indoor cat may sleep many more hours than one who goes outside at night.

All animals and humans need some sleep, but God doesn't. He doesn't have a physical body that tires like ours do. Psalm 121 tells us that God doesn't sleep. He is awake 24 hours a day, 7 days a week. He is always alert and always looking out for you.

That means that when you wake up from a bad

41

dream in the middle of the night, God knows. If you are scared by a noise in the dark, he knows. If you don't feel well, he knows. And he cares about all those things. As you lie in the dark, you can talk to him. You may even hear him speak to your heart or feel a sense of peace.

The middle of the night is a good time not only to talk to God but also to let Scripture or the words of a Christian song fill your heart and mind. The psalmist said, "Each day the LORD pours his unfailing love upon me, and through each night I sing his songs, praying to God who gives me life" (Psalm 42:8). Perhaps the psalmist, too, had trouble sleeping at times.

It's comforting to know that the heavenly King is always watching over you day and night. You can talk to him 24-7.

Next time you have trouble sleeping, open your Bible and read Psalm 42. Or read it now and see which verses stand out most to you.

22

God's Guiding You

*Do not be afraid or discouraged, for the
LORD will personally go ahead of you.*
DEUTERONOMY 31:8

In the 1800s people moved from the East or Midwest
to the West Coast, a journey of about 2,000 miles
that took up to six months. The journey was hard and
expensive. Families needed a sturdy wagon that could
withstand the rugged terrain. They needed horses,
oxen, or mules to pull the wagon, which would be
loaded down with food, cooking utensils, clothes, and
other necessities for the trip.

Traveling by wagon to the West Coast was difficult. The trip was marked with challenges like broken
wagon wheels, injured animals, illness, running out of
food or water, poor weather, and trails that were difficult to follow. Families would travel together in wagon
trains for safety and support.

Sometimes the difference between success and
failure depended solely on having an experienced trail
guide. The best guides knew the route, what dangers
lay ahead, when and where to stop for supplies or for

winter, and where to find water and animals to hunt for food.

The pioneers weren't the first group of people to make a long journey. The Israelites in Old Testament times traveled for 40 years in the wilderness. Their trip didn't need to last that long, but God made them wander 40 years because they hadn't trusted him enough to take possession of the land he'd promised them. God didn't leave them alone, though. He guided them the entire way using a cloud to lead the way in the daytime and a pillar of fire at night (see Exodus 13:21).

God still guides people today. You won't see a cloud or pillar of fire meant for you, but you may see him work out circumstances or send the right person into your life to guide you. Or he might use a book, a passage of Scripture, or a Sunday school lesson to show you the way.

Although God leads you differently today than he led the Israelites in Old Testament times, his promise is the same. He will always be with you, and he will always guide you.

God has led different people in different ways. He spoke to Moses in a burning bush and led him using a cloud and fire. What other ways did God lead people in the Bible? Think about Gideon, Esther, Daniel, and Paul. If you aren't familiar with their stories, ask a parent or Sunday school teacher to help you find them in the Bible. How does God give you direction today?

23
Your Heart's Desires

Take delight in the LORD, and he will give you your heart's desires.

PSALM 37:4

Many people like to make a list of things they want to do before they die. The items on a list of life goals are mostly one-time events, not things that will be repeated, and the things on these lists range from simple to much more complex. Someone may want to walk on the beach at sunset with a certain friend, write a poem for an old love, or visit a new place. Another person may choose to include bigger things, such as climbing Mount Fuji, hang gliding in Mexico, or writing a novel.

Many times the things on someone's list are things the person doesn't really think he or she will do. It would take a lot of planning and determination. But if people want something bad enough, they will find a way to do it.

Today's verse talks about the desires of your heart. Something you desire in your heart is different from an item written on a list of goals. Items on a life-goals list are things you want to own or do, places you want to

visit, or perhaps people you want to meet. The desires of your heart aren't like that. They are the things you want most in life, and as you learn more about God and try to follow his way, you will find that you desire the same things that God desires for you. You may begin to desire new opportunities to serve him, a way to develop the talents you'll use for him, or a new best friend who loves God as much as you do. There may even be things you haven't thought about yet.

How do you receive the desires of your heart? The first half of Psalm 37:4 says to take delight in the Lord. That means finding pleasure in learning more about God, growing closer to him, and finding your happiness in him. Sometimes God may seem far away or not as real as the people around you. It's easier to have fun hanging out with friends than spending time with God and allowing him to change you into the person he created you to be.

But in order for the second part of the verse to happen—getting your heart's desires—the first part of the verse has to take place. When you find your joy in Jesus, then your heart's desires will line up with what God has planned for you. That doesn't mean that it's wrong to want earthly things, but the more important things are the blessings God has planned for your life.

For fun, what ten things would be on your list of goals for your life? Dream big! What kinds of blessings do you think God wants to give his children?

24
Longing for God

As the deer longs for streams of water,
so I long for you, O God.
PSALM 42:1

White-tailed deer drink from wherever they can get water—streams, ponds, rivers, springs, and even mud puddles. During the winter, these deer need 1½ quarts of water per 100 pounds of weight. So if a deer weighs only 100 pounds, he needs only 1½ quarts of water each day. If he weighs 200 pounds, then he needs 3 quarts of water a day. During the summer the amount of water the deer needs doubles.

If there is a drought, it's a double problem for deer, because there isn't water to drink and food doesn't grow. Deer also get water from some of the foods they eat. During a drought, deer may have to search farther away to find enough water. The psalmist uses the example of a deer longing for water to describe his longing for God.

Have you ever been really thirsty? Perhaps you were exercising and felt like you needed a drink, or maybe you were outside when it was hot and you wanted water.

You might have gone inside and gotten a glass of water from the sink. Or maybe you had a water bottle with you and gulped all of it down. The water refreshed you.

Do you have a thirst for God's Word like the thirst you have for water on a hot day? Do you look forward to reading your Bible and soaking up its words? If reading your Bible seems like a chore, you might be making it too hard. The goal is to learn about God and become more like Jesus. One way to do that is to start in the Gospels—Matthew, Mark, Luke, and John— and read about Jesus' life here on earth. The Gospels are easier to read and understand than some other sections of the Bible. Many of the stories may already be familiar to you. If you're more experienced in reading the Bible, challenge yourself to read a section you haven't read before.

Like the psalmist, search after God's Word each day and fill your life with it.

If you've never read the Bible on your own before, choose one of the Gospels (Matthew through John) and read a few verses each day. Jot down at least one thing you learn. If you've been reading your Bible for a while, tackle an Epistle (Romans through Jude) and find one new thing from the verses you read.

25
A Good Reputation

Choose a good reputation over great riches.
PROVERBS 22:1

What is the most valuable thing in the world? One person might say gold, while another may say diamonds. One person values money, while another prefers jewels. A collector might value a rare coin more than anything else. If you ask some people what the most valuable thing in the world is, they may give an answer like family or friends. Those can't be bought with money.

What you think is most valuable depends on its worth to you. Jewels, antiques, and coins may not mean much to you. What do you consider the most valuable? What do you want more than anything else? The things you choose may be really important, but they aren't what is most important according to the wise King Solomon.

In the book of Proverbs, King Solomon says that a good reputation, or being respected for the type of person you are, is worth more than great riches. What people think of you is better than silver or gold. What people think of you is called your reputation.

What do people think when they hear your name? If someone mentions you to a teacher, does your teacher think about what a responsible and well-behaved student you are? Or does he or she think of you as someone who seeks attention in class with silly behavior? Does your church group leader think of you as someone who participates and is eager to grow spiritually or as someone who shows little interest? Do your parents think of you as the child who takes initiative in getting jobs done correctly and on time or as the one who disappears when there is work to do?

Reputations are earned over time by how you act and react, whether things are going well or are falling apart. Your character determines how you act. When people see those actions, they form a picture of you. A good reputation is worth more than money or the things it can buy. That's because it shows who you really are.

Sometimes people can fool others by their actions and earn a reputation they aren't worthy of, but God sees the heart and who a person really is.

List four words you think describe yourself. Then ask two friends, a teacher, and a parent (or any four people who vary in age and how they know you) to honestly name four words that describe you. Are any of the words the same as those you used? How do the words others listed compare with each other? How do they compare with your list? What do the words say about how others see you?

26
Hot Coals

If your enemies are hungry, feed them. If they are
thirsty, give them something to drink. In doing this,
you will heap burning coals of shame on their heads.

ROMANS 12:20

Booker T. Washington is known for founding the
Tuskegee Institute in Alabama. As an African
American, he was often treated unfairly by people who
looked different from him and judged him only by the
color of his skin.

Booker T. Washington could have easily hated
the people who treated him wrongly. But he didn't.
He said, "I shall allow no man to belittle my soul by
making me hate him." In other words, he wasn't going
to let someone else's actions cause him to react in
a mean way. He knew he couldn't stop how people
treated him because of the color of his skin, but he
could control his own reactions to their unkindness.

In today's verse, the apostle Paul told the Christians in Rome to go a step further and treat their
enemies with kindness. This wasn't a new thought. Paul
was repeating words penned years earlier by the wise
King Solomon: "If your enemies are hungry, give them

food to eat. If they are thirsty, give them water to drink. You will heap burning coals of shame on their heads, and the LORD will reward you" (Proverbs 25:21-22).

What does today's verse mean for you? You probably don't have any real enemies. But you might have someone in your life who is hard to like. Maybe she makes fun of you every chance she gets. Not only that, but she gets her friends to do the same. It would be very tempting to say something mean back to her, but the right thing to do is react with kindness. Not because she deserves to be treated kindly but because you're God's princess, and nothing she says can change that.

You may be thinking that answer is too simple. Even though you know you are important to God, it might be nice to have other people recognize your worth. They will, but it just might not be right now. The only thing you can control is your reaction to their mean-girl tactics. Don't give them the victory by letting them get to you. Make the right choice, and respond to them God's way—with kindness.

React in kindness to those who are hard to like. Smile and walk on by when you'd rather get back at them. Memorize either Romans 12:20 or Proverbs 25:21-22, and quote it to yourself as a reminder when others act ugly.

27
God's Gifts

God has given each of you a gift from his great variety of spiritual gifts. Use them well to serve one another.

1 PETER 4:10

Birthdays and Christmas are often celebrated by giving gifts. Many times the gifts are in different-sized packages, wrapped in special paper and tied with ribbon. Part of the fun is trying to guess what's in the package and then opening it to find out. Did you get the camera you wanted? Or is it a watch in that package? Is there a pair of new jeans or a jacket inside the gift bag?

God has given you gifts too. These aren't gifts like a tablet or a bicycle. They are things you are good at doing. He wants you to use your talents to help or encourage others. Can you think of any gifts you have that allow you to do good for others?

You may be surprised to find out that your natural friendliness is one of God's gifts to you. It helps you to reach out to other girls and make them feel welcome at church or feel they have a friend at school. Your tendency to listen to others is God's gift to you so you can encourage a discouraged student,

brother or sister, teacher, or parent. Your talent for writing is God's gift to you, allowing you to jot an uplifting note to a friend, Sunday school teacher, or lunchroom worker. The organizational skills you have that drive your sister crazy when you hang her clothes by color might be just the gift you need to help organize a mission fund-raiser.

What seems to you to be merely a part of your personality may be something God has gifted you with in order to do something special for him. He wants you to make a difference in the lives of those around you. So be happy that your talents are things like being friendly, listening, putting things in order, or whatever skills you might have in doing good. God gave you exactly what you need to use each day to do good things for others.

Make a list of all the things you're good at. Include the things that seem little, like the ability to smile even when things are going wrong or the way you can find something good in every situation. The way your dog prefers you to others might mean he senses a compassionate spirit. Put that on the list too. If you can't think of anything, have a parent or teacher help you. Then ask God to show you how to use those things to make a difference in someone else's life.

28

Run the Race

*Since we are surrounded by such a huge crowd
of witnesses to the life of faith, let us strip off
every weight that slows us down, especially the
sin that so easily trips us up. And let us run with
endurance the race God has set before us.*

HEBREWS 12:1

Running marathons is a popular activity. You may have heard of the Honolulu Marathon in Honolulu, Hawaii; the Bank of America Marathon in Chicago, Illinois; the Boston Marathon in Boston, Massachusetts; and the Walt Disney World Marathon in Orlando, Florida. Marathon runners push themselves to prove they can run 26 miles and successfully cross the finish line. In order to do that, they must stay motivated, train for months, and take care of their bodies. Failing to do any of those things will make the trek to the finish line harder or even impossible.

What does a marathon have to do with you, God's princess? The author of Hebrews compares the Christian life to a race. You've probably run a race on field day at school, but those races are different because they are usually short distances like 50 yards

or 100 yards. For short runs, you sprint, or run as fast as you can, over a short distance. In a marathon you must pace yourself to make sure you don't run out of energy before you hit the finish line.

The Christian life is more like a marathon than a sprint. It starts the day you give Jesus your life, and it lasts until you go home to heaven. That's more than just a spiritual sprint. It's a long-distance run, so it's important to allow God to build you up daily and prepare you for what's ahead. You can do that by reading some of the Bible each day. You can listen carefully in Sunday school and church and pick out at least one thing that you can use during the coming week in your spiritual marathon. You may want to read a Christian book such as a missionary's biography or a book about living for Jesus.

It's also important when you run to get rid of extra weight. Running a marathon is not the time to wear ankle weights. Running the Christian race is much easier without the weight of sins like anger, jealousy, gossip, or dishonesty. Ditch those weights so they don't drag you down.

Ask God to prepare you for the spiritual marathon you're on. Take time to build yourself up spiritually through the Bible and church so you'll finish strong.

Ask a friend, parent, or sibling to run a mile with you this week. As you run, talk about how the Christian life is like a marathon.

29
What Should I Wear?

*Since God chose you to be the holy people he loves,
you must clothe yourselves with tenderhearted mercy,
kindness, humility, gentleness, and patience.*

COLOSSIANS 3:12

Do you like trying new clothing styles? There are a lot of styles to choose from, and new clothing is being designed each day. You can go to an expensive store and buy new designer fashions that are modeled on the runways in New York or Paris, or you can put together secondhand clothing items bought in a thrift shop to create a cute new outfit just for you. Clothes are an important part of life. If you opened your closet, you might see shoes, jackets, sports uniforms, swimming suits, clothes for playing in, uniforms for school, and clothes to wear for church. Worldwide, people spend close to $180 billion on children's clothing each year!

The Bible doesn't say much about the clothes you wear, but God does want you to be modest and to honor him in everything you do, including what you wear. The Bible also mentions what God wants you to clothe your spirit with. According to today's verse,

the characteristics of tenderhearted mercy, kindness, humility, gentleness, and patience should cover you just as your physical clothing covers your body.

How can you clothe yourself with godly characteristics? By asking God to help you face each day with your heart filled with those things. When you're tempted to get angry, take a deep breath and remind yourself of the compassionate way to react. When you are jealous, step back and allow yourself to put others' needs and desires ahead of your own. When you are impatient, count to ten, and allow yourself to relax and respond with patience.

God doesn't expect you to be able to do it on your own, and he's waiting to help you.

Write the words *tenderhearted mercy, kindness, humility, gentleness,* and *patience* on an index card. Place it where you will see it as you get dressed each morning. While you put on your clothes for the day, ask God to clothe your spirit with each of these characteristics.

30
The Big Three

Feel free to take notes that you can look back on if you feel unloved

God has not given us a spirit of fear and timidity,
but of power, love, and self-discipline.

2 TIMOTHY 1:7

When you are on the front lines of a battle, you need to be prepared. You must know the plan and have your weapon ready. You need to know where to be and when to move. You must know the enemy you're up against and be prepared to defeat him or her. The same is true in the Christian life, because you may find yourself on the front lines for Jesus.

The apostle Paul wrote several letters to Timothy, who was the young pastor of the church in Ephesus. Paul wanted to encourage Timothy because Timothy was sometimes looked down on for being young and was picked on by those who didn't like Christians. Timothy was on the front lines of service to God, and Paul wanted Timothy to realize he didn't have to fear the mean people or be timid because God had given him everything he needed to succeed—power, love, and self-discipline. Each of those things is important on its own, but the three together are unbeatable.

There have been powerful men and women in

history, but true power isn't the ability to control others. The power Paul is talking about is the ability God gives us to love and serve others. Remember when Jesus met with his disciples in the upper room? He was God in the flesh, but he washed their feet. Jesus used his powerful position to serve and minister to others. There are people today who serve God through his power. They are building wells in poor countries, honoring Jesus on the football field, taking the gospel and medicine to remote parts of the world, organizing Bible studies, and more.

Having power to do things is good, especially if you do them out of love. Because God loved you first, you can love others. There may be people in your life who are hard to love, but as God's princess you have his love filling you up and helping you to love others.

Self-discipline goes hand in hand with power and love. Having self-discipline means not being controlled by the temptation to do things but letting God control your desires so that you will make good choices.

Each day is an opportunity to seek out God, to ask him to show you what he wants you to do, and to rely on his power, love, and self-discipline to do it.

Can you think of some great leaders, pastors, missionaries, or athletes who live out God's plan for them with power, love, and self-discipline? How are they changing their world? Ask God to help you make a difference too.

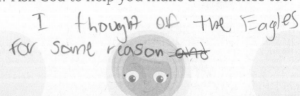
I thought of the Eagles
for some reason and

31

No Worries

*Don't worry about anything; instead, pray
about everything. Tell God what you need, and
thank him for all he has done. Then you will
experience God's peace, which exceeds anything
we can understand. His peace will guard your
hearts and minds as you live in Christ Jesus.*

PHILIPPIANS 4:6-7

Do you ever worry about things? Maybe you worry about fitting in, experiencing the changes happening to your body, facing a new school, completing your homework, taking the yearly achievement test at school, being deserted by your friends, arguing with your brothers and sisters, or having the right clothes. Worrying can be overwhelming if you allow it to be.

The problem with worry is that it's a thief. It robs you of your sleep. Then you go to school tired and grouchy. It robs you of your happiness and peace. It even saps your energy and takes away your enthusiasm for activities you normally look forward to. Worry can also make your stomach or head hurt.

The good thing is that you don't have to live with worry. Today's verses have the key to defeating it.

Instead of getting anxious about things, talk to God. Share with him how you feel. He already knows what you're worried about, but he wants to hear it from you. And he wants to give you peace in place of the worry. Talking to God about the things that bother you doesn't mean they'll all disappear. It means that God will be with you as you face the situations. He'll help you know how to handle them, and he will fill you with his peace in spite of the things that make you anxious.

When you talk to God about the class that seems too hard, the girl who targets you with her meanness, or the upcoming oral presentation you have to give, ask him to guide you to the right person to talk to about it—a parent, a church leader, a teacher, or a school counselor. Talking with God and a trusted adult can help you feel more hopeful and give you peace.

The peace that God offers you keeps your heart and mind calm and draws you close to him. It guards you from worry so that you can live each day the best you can.

List the things that worry you. Talk to God about them, and then seek out a trusted adult to talk to. Keep praying and talking until the anxiety has gone away and you're ready to face each day with hope.

32
A Changed Life

Anyone who belongs to Christ has become a new person. The old life is gone; a new life has begun!

2 CORINTHIANS 5:17

Have you ever read *The Very Hungry Caterpillar* by Eric Carle? What makes the story fun is reading about the food the caterpillar eats each day. After two weeks he chews his way out, but he's not a caterpillar anymore. He's a beautiful butterfly.

Have you seen a caterpillar turn into a butterfly? Maybe your teacher brought a caterpillar into your classroom, and you watched it become a chrysalis and then emerge as a butterfly. The caterpillar that once spent its life on the ground can now fly, bringing a bit of color to the sky.

When you made the decision to follow Jesus, he changed your life. God's work in making you into a new person is similar to the change that happens to a caterpillar. God knew you before you were born, and you were wonderfully designed by him (see Psalm 139:14). When you were born, you were like the caterpillar. You weren't yet all God wanted you to be.

But on the day you made the decision to follow

Jesus, God took away your sin nature and replaced it with a new nature. He gave you a desire to please him. You became a new person on the inside.

That doesn't mean that you'll never be tempted to sin. You will. But God's Spirit lives within you and gives you the strength to overcome temptation. And if you choose to give in, he'll nudge your conscience and let you know that what you did was wrong.

Maybe you are still a caterpillar. If you haven't yet asked Jesus to be your Savior, he's waiting for you. He wants to take away your sins and change your heart. He will transform you into a beautiful butterfly.

Read *The Very Hungry Caterpillar* or a book about butterflies to a younger sibling, or read it to yourself. Tell someone you know about the day Jesus changed your heart.

33
God's Laws

The commandments of the LORD are right, bringing joy to the heart. The commands of the LORD are clear, giving insight for living. . . . They are more desirable than gold, even the finest gold. They are sweeter than honey, even honey dripping from the comb.

PSALM 19:8, 10

Laws have changed over the years. Some laws from long ago don't make much sense today. For instance, in Missouri it's illegal to drive with an uncaged bear in your car. Does that make you wonder how many people were driving around with bears in their cars before that law was passed? If you like arcade games, you might want to know that in South Carolina it's illegal to play pinball unless you're 18 years old. And if you live in Salem, West Virginia, you'd better control your sweet tooth on Sundays. It's illegal there to eat candy less than 1½ hours before church. And don't get out your marbles, dominoes, and yo-yos on Sunday. In several states, those are illegal on the Lord's Day.

Chances are most people have forgotten that these laws exist, much less follow them. But God's laws are a different matter. No, you don't have to follow all the laws given to the Israelites in the Old Testament book of Leviticus. Many of those were written for that time period and would be very difficult to follow today. The laws about sacrifices for sin ended when Jesus gave himself as the final sacrifice for our salvation. But there are still things God wants you to do. Some of them are obeying your parents, loving those who aren't easy to love, giving part of your money in the offering, and telling the truth.

Even though Christians today aren't under Old Testament law, they should obey the Word of God. Doing what God wants shouldn't be difficult. When you love God, you want to do what he asks. God's princesses should desire to follow God's ways. The psalmist David said that God's commands bring joy to the heart and insight for living. Who doesn't want those?

Look up Psalm 19 in your own Bible. Read the whole psalm, and jot down what it says about God's Word, laws, or commands. How does it apply to you today?

34
One Life

[Jesus] died for everyone so that those who receive his new life will no longer live for themselves. Instead, they will live for Christ, who died and was raised for them.

2 CORINTHIANS 5:15

Missionary C. T. Studd was born into a wealthy family in England in 1860. By the time he was 16 years old, he was an expert cricket player. (Cricket is an English sport played with a bat and a ball.) C. T. had everything going for him, but he gave up his comfortable life for God.

Giving away a large sum of money he'd inherited, C. T. dedicated himself to sharing the gospel in China, India, and Africa. He lived out the words of today's verse. He was willing to turn his back on an easy life to serve God as a missionary. C. T. Studd had a motto he lived by: "If Jesus Christ is God and died for me, then no sacrifice can be too great for me to make for Him."

God calls everyone to follow him, but he doesn't call all of us to follow him in the same way. For C. T. Studd, following God meant being a full-time missionary. God has called others to be pastors, doctors, nurses, soccer players, teachers, sanitation

workers, waitresses, computer technicians, stay-at-home moms, and more. The Lord needs people in all areas of life who will share the gospel with the people they see each day.

You don't need to wait to be an adult to share the good news of Jesus with those around you. Your mission field is right where you are today. The people you encounter need Jesus just as much as people in a foreign land do. Sure, anyone in our country can buy a Bible, and there are churches all over, but that doesn't mean people will read a Bible or go to church on their own. The students you pass in the hallway at school or in your homeschool group, the players on your sports team, the student who takes music lessons right after you—any of those may need you to share your faith with them.

Today's verse says those who believe in Jesus should live their lives for him, but it doesn't say how. God can use each person right where he or she is. Ask him to show you how you can live for him right now.

Look around you. How can you share your faith with those you encounter? Is there someone next to you in class or at lunch who might need to hear about Jesus? Is there someone you could invite to church? Ask God to show you who needs to hear about him.

35
Loving Those Who Are Hard to Love

We love each other because he loved us first.

1 JOHN 4:19

God wants us to love others because he loved us first. Before you were born, God loved you. God showed his love for you when he created you, and he sent his Son Jesus to die for you so that you could be one of his princesses. He shows his love for you every day by giving you life and all the things you need. God's love never changes, so you can count on him to love you no matter what happens at school, at home, with your friends, or with your family.

Because God loves you, he wants you to love others. This isn't always easy, because there are people in life who are harder to love. Just think about the neighborhood bully who hurts others or the girl who makes fun of your hair or clothes. Or maybe there's someone at church who seems a little different. There might be a neighbor who yells at you when your softball lands in her yard or your cat uses her yard as a shortcut. It might not be easy to love these

people, but sometimes they are the people who need love the most.

God created all people in his image, even those who are more difficult to love. So everyone is equal in his sight. God sent Jesus to die for everyone's sins because no one was really deserving of love, but God chose to show his love for the whole world by offering salvation to everyone. That's why he wants you to love everybody.

One way to show love for others, even those who are difficult to love, is by serving them. Jesus served by washing his disciples' feet at the Last Supper (see John 13). He did this even though he knew that one of them would betray him and others would run and hide instead of staying with him when he was arrested in the garden. Jesus loved his disciples anyway.

There are simple ways to serve others throughout the day. You can help someone with a math assignment or help him find a book in the school library. You can offer to carry something for a friend when her arms are full, or pick up something that is dropped. You can collect trash at lunch or do a chore for someone. The important thing is to do it out of love for the other person because of God's love for you.

Think of someone who is hard for you to love. What makes this person hard to love? How can you serve him or her today in order to demonstrate God's love?

36
The Golden Rule

[Jesus said,] "Do to others whatever you would like them to do to you. This is the essence of all that is taught in the law and the prophets."

MATTHEW 7:12

You've likely heard the Golden Rule ever since you were small. Someone probably told you, "Do to others as you would have them do to you" or "Treat others the way you want them to treat you." These are simply other ways of saying today's verse. That makes Jesus the first person to say what we know as the Golden Rule.

Many times people use that rule to mean you shouldn't treat someone badly if that person treats you badly. For instance, if someone trips you while you're walking down the hall, don't look for a chance to trip him or her in return. If someone is rude to you, don't be rude back. While it's good to avoid getting even when someone treats you unfairly or unkindly, Jesus' words mean more than that. They are a call to action.

Think of it this way. You see an unpopular boy get pushed from behind. Everything he's carrying goes flying. You might think, *Wow. I'd never treat anyone like*

that, because I'd hate to be treated like that. That's good. But what's better is to look at the poor kid picking up his stuff and ask yourself, *If that were me, what would I want someone to do for me?* You'd want help picking up your stuff, and maybe you'd want someone to say something encouraging to help you feel better about the situation. In that case, that's what you should do for the boy.

Don't just avoid getting even with others. Jesus wants his princesses to step out and take action. How would that look in your life? It would mean looking around and seeing the needs of people. Does your mom look tired while she's preparing dinner? If you were your mom, what would you want someone to do for you? Help you set the table? Help you peel the potatoes? Go ahead and do it for her. Is your little brother struggling with his math? If that were you, what would you want someone to do for you? Explain it to you? Help you do a couple of the problems? Sit by you as you do the homework? Do that for him.

You may not always feel like doing the right thing. It may mean going out of your way, helping when you don't feel like it, or doing more work when you were all ready to have fun or relax. Just consider it your job as a princess, and do it for Jesus.

Look for someone with a need. Ask yourself what you'd want someone to do for you in that situation, and then go do it. Keep a Golden Rule journal this week, and write down one way you lived it out each day.

37
Purity

Dear friends, we are already God's children, but he has not yet shown us what we will be like when Christ appears. But we do know that we will be like him, for we will see him as he really is. And all who have this eager expectation will keep themselves pure, just as he is pure.

1 JOHN 3:2-3

If you live in a place that's cold in the winter, you know the beauty of freshly fallen snow, especially when big, soft flakes coat the ground and bare tree branches with a blanket of white. Things that usually look dingy are bright white with the blanket of newly fallen snow. That's what God's forgiveness is like. Isaiah 1:18 says, "'Come now, let's settle this,' says the LORD. 'Though your sins are like scarlet, I will make them as white as snow. Though they are red like crimson, I will make them as white as wool.'" God cleanses a person's heart and frees it from sin. He makes a person's heart pure.

In today's verses, God tells us to keep ourselves pure after we've been forgiven. When God tells his princesses to stay pure, he means that they should avoid sin.

One thing that helps keep you pure is being careful about the things you see and hear. Images you see on movies or television shows stay in your mind. So do song lyrics. When they are about things that don't honor God, they pollute you. When you choose to say things that are unkind or rude or act in ways that don't show God's love, that pollutes you. It's very important to guard your heart from things that don't bring God glory. If you aren't sure what things honor God, just imagine how you'd feel if he walked in and saw what you were doing. Would he be pleased? Would he tell you, "Good job"? Or would you cringe in embarrassment?

Remember the freshly fallen snow? How does it look after cars have driven on it? After people have walked on it? It no longer looks fresh and pure. That's what happens when someone allows sin into her life. The purity is replaced by sin and guilt, and the whiteness turns dingy.

You can avoid that by asking God to help you honor him in what you say and what you do. That's a prayer he loves to answer.

Find a picture of freshly fallen snow in a magazine or online, or draw one yourself. Tape it where you will see it each day so it can remind you to ask God to guide your choices and keep you pure.

38
A Shining Light

[Jesus said,] "You are the light of the world—like a city on a hilltop that cannot be hidden. . . . Let your good deeds shine out for all to see, so that everyone will praise your heavenly Father."

MATTHEW 5:14, 16

On the last night of mission camp, each camper was given an unlit candle. All the lights were extinguished in the big-top tent so everyone was sitting in the dark. Then one of the camp counselors lit a candle. This candle represented the light of Jesus. Even though the candle was small, it shone brightly because everything around it was dark. If the lights had been on, the lone lit candle wouldn't have been seen. But because the tent was dark, the single light shone brightly.

The first camp counselor lit the candle of the next counselor to symbolize sharing the light of the gospel. The second counselor then lit the candle of a third counselor, and so on, until all the counselors had lit candles. By the light of those few candles, the campers could dimly see those gathered in the tent. Each counselor lit the candle of a camper, and each camper in turn lit the candle of the camper next to him or her,

until everyone was holding a lit candle. The whole tent was ablaze with candlelight.

But the light of the candles wasn't meant to stay in the tent. The light of God's Word, the salvation message, is meant to be shared. The campers carefully walked out of the tent, single file, by candlelight and headed to a bus to leave for their summer mission projects. During the projects, their lives would be a light for those who didn't believe in God or hadn't heard about him.

God has called you to be a light for him too. You don't have to leave on a mission trip to do that. Your life can shine brightly right where you are. Each time you say a kind word or cheerfully help someone, the love of Jesus shines through you. Each time you smile in encouragement or put someone's needs ahead of your own, your light is shining.

Remember, even a lone candle flame lights up the dark. Shine your light for Jesus this week.

Try the candle lighting for yourself. Ask a parent to get a candle for each family member who is old enough to safely hold a lit candle. Wait until dark, and then go outside, away from streetlights. Have a parent light the candles one at a time. How much difference does a single candle make? How about when they are all lit? What happens if you spread out, each person going to a different corner of the yard? Talk about ways you can shine for Jesus individually and as a family.

39
The Right Path

Trust in the L{ord} with all your heart; do not depend on your own understanding. Seek his will in all you do, and he will show you which path to take.

P{roverbs} 3:5-6

In the famous poem "The Road Not Taken" by Robert Frost, the traveler tells of coming upon two roads in the woods. Both were equally worn and covered with leaves. There was no way for the traveler to know where each road would lead. Realizing he couldn't take both, the man had to choose one road to take.

As you grow up, there will be many times when you will have to make a hard decision and choose which "road" to take. Should you go to church camp or visit your grandmother? Should you take choir or band at school? Should you sign up to spend Saturday mornings with the youth group doing service projects or sign up for the soccer league?

It might be easier if God used road signs like the ones drivers follow—no U-turn, right turn only, or straight ahead. He doesn't use those kinds of signs, but he may send a Sunday school teacher into your life to help guide you. Or the pastor might say exactly what

you need to hear to understand what God wants you to do. God may speak to you in your heart, or he may open the doors for some opportunities and close the doors for others.

Today's verses are saying that it's important to seek out God's plan for you in all you do. When you read the Bible, ask God for wisdom in knowing what his plan is, and try to do the things you already know he wants you to do. He'll lead you down the right path for you. This doesn't mean you can't take important steps in making good choices. Talking to parents or other trusted adults along with looking at the possible consequences of each choice is a good way to make decisions too.

You may wonder if you'll recognize God's leading and make the right choices, but that's where trusting God comes in. If he wants you to do something, and you are willing to do the things he asks of you, he'll make sure you're on the right path.

What decisions are in your future? Start asking God now to lead you in the right direction. Remember that he may use the Bible, a pastor, a parent, or another godly person to help guide you.

40
A Fulfilling Life

[Jesus said,] "The thief's purpose is to steal and kill and destroy. My purpose is to give [my sheep] a rich and satisfying life. I am the good shepherd. The good shepherd sacrifices his life for the sheep."

JOHN 10:10-11

When Jesus lived on the earth, he taught people using illustrations or stories that were about things they understood. He talked about planting seeds and growing crops. He talked about candles and salt. He also spoke of sheep to illustrate his teachings, because that was something the people understood. Shepherding was one of the main occupations of the Israelites in the Old Testament, and in the New Testament shepherds were among the first to visit baby Jesus when he was born.

Jesus told the people that a true shepherd calls his sheep and they come to him because they know his voice (see John 10:2-3). He also said a shepherd would sacrifice his life for his sheep. He told them that he was the Good Shepherd, and that he had come so that people could have a rich and satisfying life. Some versions of the Bible call it abundant life.

Jesus didn't mean that people who believed in him would become rich with money and possessions. He wasn't promising they'd have the best of everything that life had to offer. His promise wasn't about things you can own and buy. It was about having a personal relationship with him and a better life by knowing and loving him. Because Jesus, the Good Shepherd, sacrificed his life for everyone's sins, life has purpose.

Having the newest game system, all the latest movies, or a big allowance might seem like a desirable goal, but money can't buy the things that matter the most—peace, purpose, and contentment. Those things come by knowing the Good Shepherd and being one of his sheep. When you do that, you have a fulfilling life here and a future with Jesus in heaven.

Look up sheep on the Internet or in a book, and try to find out five facts about sheep and shepherds. Do any of them apply to you and your Good Shepherd? How?

41
Press On

I focus on this one thing: Forgetting the past and looking forward to what lies ahead, I press on to reach the end of the race and receive the heavenly prize for which God, through Christ Jesus, is calling us.

<small>PHILIPPIANS 3:13-14</small>

On August 7, 1954, more than 35,000 spectators gathered in Empire Stadium in Vancouver, British Columbia, for the British Empire and Commonwealth Games. On this day a race was run that became known as the Miracle Mile. British medical student and former Olympian Roger Bannister had been the first person to run the mile in under four minutes just three months before the Commonwealth Games. At this race, he was going to run again against seven other runners.

John Landy of Australia had the lead during the race. But on the final turn of the last lap, he looked back over his left shoulder. Bannister passed him on the right and crossed the finish line first. It was the first race where two runners finished the mile in under four minutes.

The apostle Paul knew that the way to finish a race strong was to look forward and press toward

the finish line. Looking back at past mistakes slows forward progress, and it can cause a person to stumble and fall. Paul determined that the bad choices in his past wouldn't stop him from looking forward and reaching his goal—to be with Jesus for eternity.

Does that mean that you can't ever think about things in the past? No. But it's easy to get caught up in what could have been or to be held back by bitterness over things that have already happened. It's good to learn from earlier mistakes and victories but not to live in the past.

Before Paul came to know Christ, he was known for persecuting Christians. He was even on his way to persecute the Christians in Damascus when Jesus stopped him in his tracks and Paul turned to the Savior. If Paul had dwelled on the bad things he'd done before he met Jesus, that would have hindered Paul's work of spreading the gospel. So he accepted Jesus' forgiveness and focused on the goal in front of him.

It's easy to think about past mistakes and problems. But don't dwell on them. Learn from them and let them go. Like Paul, strive forward toward the finish line—being with Jesus.

Have you watched a track meet? If not, try to watch a race in person or online and see how the runners concentrate on the finish line. How can you have that same focus in your Christian life?

42
Recharging

Jesus said, "Let's go off by ourselves to a quiet place and rest awhile." . . . So they left by boat for a quiet place, where they could be alone.

MARK 6:31-32

Jesus sent his disciples out to tell people about God. He also gave them power to cast out evil spirits and heal the sick. The disciples traveled around doing what Jesus had asked them to do. When they returned from their ministry journey, the disciples shared with Jesus what they had done. But while they were trying to talk with Jesus, people were still coming to him, wanting to hear him and to be healed. So many people kept coming that Jesus and the disciples didn't even have time to stop and eat, much less rest. So Jesus said, "Let's go off by ourselves to a quiet place and rest awhile."

The disciples had been doing good things that Jesus had asked them to do. But after their ministry journey, the 12 men were weary from the work of sharing the Good News and healing people.

You probably have things in your house that need to be charged, such as a cell phone, an MP3 player, a laptop, or a battery-operated toy or game. When the battery is low or runs down, the device or toy no longer works. You can't make a call with the phone, you can't listen to music on the MP3 player, and you can't play with the toy or game. It needs to be plugged in and recharged.

That's how the disciples were after their ministry trip. They were run down and needed to recharge. Their minds and bodies needed rest. Spending time away with Jesus would help them do this.

As you're doing good each day and sharing the gospel message with others, it's important for you to take time to recharge too.

God wants you to tell others about him and to help others, but if you're constantly giving to people and not taking time to fill yourself with God's Word or to spend time with other Christians, you may find yourself drained spiritually.

Find time to read the Bible and pray. Read books about living for Christ, praying, or knowing more about God. Listen in church, and look for ways the message applies to you.

When you take time to recharge, you will have more energy and excitement later to get back to work for God.

Take a look at how much time you spend giving of yourself to others and doing things for God. Are you taking time to recharge? How? If not, what things can you do this week to recharge your spiritual batteries?

43
Choosing What's Best

You say, "I am allowed to do anything"—
but not everything is good for you. And
even though "I am allowed to do anything,"
I must not become a slave to anything.

1 CORINTHIANS 6:12

How much "screen time" do you have each day? Think about all the time you spend on your cell phone, MP3 player, tablet, game system, computer, or television. The average 8- to 18-year-old in the United States spends seven to eight hours a day on electronic devices. That's about the same amount of time that you spend in school or that your parents work each day.

Is there anything wrong with using a cell phone or a computer? Not in itself. Both of those things can be helpful in learning new things. With your computer, you can do research for your school classes, type in class notes, read about missionaries around the world, and even e-mail them. You can read the Bible online in many different versions.

There are many activities or possessions that aren't wrong in themselves, but they become wrong because of how they are used. The apostle Paul said

he was allowed to do anything, but not everything was good for him. (Of course he didn't mean things that are forbidden by God.) He also said he wouldn't let anything control him.

Some things that are beneficial can also become addicting or control your time or your money. Researching topics on the Internet helps you learn and use your brain, but Internet use can also get out of control if you become obsessed with it. Playing a video game might be a fun way to spend time with a brother or sister, but if you spend your homework time doing it, or if you can't seem to stop until you hit the next level, you might be addicted.

God doesn't have a long list of dos and don'ts about your electronics—or other activities—but he has given you guidelines to help you make the best choices. Think about what Paul wrote in 1 Corinthians 6 as you choose how to spend your time this week.

Try keeping a log of how you spend your time. Pay attention to what you do each day, and jot down how much time you spend: being in school, doing homework, helping around the house, reading your Bible and praying, attending church, using electronic gadgets, playing outside, and volunteering. Add up your time at the end of the week. Do you need to make some changes? How does your time chart reflect what's most important to you?

44
God's Recipe

*Always be joyful. Never stop praying. Be
thankful in all circumstances, for this is God's
will for you who belong to Christ Jesus.*

1 Thessalonians 5:16-18

What would make you truly happy? Would it be not having math homework for a week? Or the chance to go on a fun vacation? How about getting to buy anything you want? Those things might make you happy, but the happiness would fade once the excitement of getting something or taking a trip wore off. Happiness is good, but joy is better.

Happiness is an emotion that changes depending on your feelings. When things are going well, you feel happy. Joy is beyond that. It's an inner feeling that depends on God, not on things, situations, or people.

Paul told the Christians in Thessalonica to always be joyful because their joy came from knowing God and accepting Jesus' gift of salvation. Paul gave them two more instructions—keep praying, and be thankful no matter what's happening. These three actions— being joyful, praying about your needs, and thanking God—work together. If you are praying and thanking

God for the things he's given you, the joy flows from your heart. If you're joyful inside, it's easier to be thankful and to pray.

It's good to have a special time when you pray, but it's also good to say short prayers throughout the day. Pray for your teachers, tests, and school situations as you ride the bus to school. Pray for your friends as you see them in the hallway. Say a prayer in your heart when you hear of a particular need.

In addition to being joyful and praying, God wants you to be thankful for the things he has given you. Sometimes it's easy to overlook your blessings because you take them for granted. Things like a house, clothing, and food seem commonplace, but there are people who don't always have those things. The very things you take for granted just might be what other people are hoping for!

Ask God to fill your heart with his joy. Keep your heart connected to him through prayer. And thank him for the things he's given you.

Write the words *joy, prayer*, and *thanksgiving* on separate index cards. Look up Philippians 4:4 and write it on the back of the joy card. Write three things you want to remember to pray for on the back of the prayer card. And write at least three things you are thankful for on the back of the thanksgiving card. Put them where you will see them often as a reminder of the three things you should do.

45
Mirror, Mirror, on the Wall

Don't just listen to God's word. You must do what it says. Otherwise, you are only fooling yourselves. For if you listen to the word and don't obey, it is like glancing at your face in a mirror. You see yourself, walk away, and forget what you look like. But if you look carefully into the perfect law that sets you free, and if you do what it says and don't forget what you heard, then God will bless you for doing it.

JAMES 1:22-25

The German fairy tale "Snow White" features a magic mirror. In the story, the queen gives birth to a baby girl, Snow White. The queen dies, and the king marries again a year later. The new queen is vain and daily asks her mirror, "Mirror, mirror, on the wall, who's the fairest one of all?" The mirror always answers that the new queen is the most beautiful in the land—until one day when the mirror informs the queen, "My queen, you may be the fairest here, but Snow White is a thousand times more fair." The queen doesn't like this answer. But she knows the mirror can't lie, so she decides to get rid of Snow White. If you are familiar with the story, you know the queen doesn't succeed, but she certainly tries.

The apostle James talked about a mirror in the Bible book that shares his name. He said that when people read God's Word but don't obey it, it's like looking at themselves in a mirror, leaving, and forgetting what they really look like.

Suppose you read some verses that talk about putting others first. Later you see that your mom is trying to cook dinner, take care of your younger brother, and set the table all at the same time. You know from your Bible reading that you should put her first by helping her with her needs, but you really want to relax and watch television. You tell yourself you deserve a break because school was really tough. Besides, you figure your mom is used to doing all the work. You fail to obey what you know God wants you to do. James said that's the same as looking into the mirror and then going away and forgetting what you look like.

God's Word has lots of instructions for his princesses, and it's important not only to read those but also to ask God to help you obey them even when it's difficult.

Write today's verses on a card, and put it in your Bible. Use it as a reminder to not only read but also obey God's Word.

46
Kindness

Be kind to each other, tenderhearted, forgiving one another, just as God through Christ has forgiven you.

EPHESIANS 4:32

Did you know that there's a World Kindness Day? This day, dedicated to acts of kindness big and small, is celebrated on November 13 in many countries. If you haven't heard of it, that's not surprising. Most people haven't. But if you look on the Internet, there are websites devoted to it. The websites even have ideas for ways to show kindness, including giving care packs to the homeless, collecting coats for needy families, donating books to the library, reading to a young child or an elderly person, taking supplies to the local chapter of the Humane Society, and writing a thank-you card to the fire department.

God doesn't have one day devoted to kindness. He wants you, his princess, to show kindness every day. He wants you to have a tender heart that's filled with kindness and forgiveness. If your heart is holding bitterness or resentment toward someone, you can't really be happy. Resentment robs you of your joy and replaces it with bad feelings instead.

The key to having good relationships with friends, family, and peers is to forgive mistakes and hurts rather than dwell on them or feel sorry for yourself. Don't think up ways to repay someone with unkindness. On your own it might be hard to show kindness instead of holding a grudge when you've been wronged, but God can help you with that. He freely forgives you, so he's more than willing to help you do that for others.

When your heart is filled with feelings of kindness and forgiveness, every day can be Kindness Day.

Make this week Kindness Week for you. Write down one thing you will do each day to be nice to another person. You might do a chore for a sibling or a parent, pick up trash at school, rake the yard for a neighbor, say something nice to the first three people you see at school, or make a card for a janitor at your church. Maybe you can involve your whole family and bake cookies for the bus driver or a Sunday school teacher, take your old towels to the Humane Society for the pet kennels, or think up another project that shows kindness.

47
God's Ambassadors

God was in Christ, reconciling the world to himself, no longer counting people's sins against them. And he gave us this wonderful message of reconciliation. So we are Christ's ambassadors; God is making his appeal through us. We speak for Christ when we plead, "Come back to God!"

2 CORINTHIANS 5:19-20

Here's a pop quiz: Do you know what an American ambassador is? If you guessed that it's an American who lives and works in another country while representing the United States, you're right. The president selects ambassadors, but the Senate must approve them. In order to be chosen as ambassadors, people need to be familiar with their country's politics and laws as well as the politics and laws of the country they will work in. Successful ambassadors will need to be able to follow the manners of another country while representing their home country in a sensitive and thoughtful way.

Paul said that he was an ambassador for Christ and that his home was in heaven. But Paul had never been to heaven. Even though Paul had not been to

heaven, when he spoke of his real home, that is where he meant. He told the church in Philippi, "We are citizens of heaven, where the Lord Jesus Christ lives. And we are eagerly waiting for him to return as our Savior" (Philippians 3:20). Although Paul lived on the earth, God called him to be an ambassador of Jesus and of heaven to people on the earth. You have the same call. You represent Jesus to the people around you.

What does this mean for you as God's princess? Just like an American ambassador should know the laws of his or her home country, you need to be familiar with the laws and manners of your country of citizenship—heaven. Learn all you can about God and his Word. Try to learn new things from the Bible. Instead of reading Bible storybooks, read your Bible. Start by reading the Epistles, which were letters to people or churches telling them how God wanted them to live. (You'll find the Epistles in the New Testament in the Bible—Romans through Jude.)

Even though heaven is your true home, God calls you to be his ambassador here on earth. Accept the challenge, and learn to be the best representative of Jesus that you can be.

Research the job of an ambassador. Who were some of the most successful ambassadors? What made them successful? How can you apply those things to your job as an ambassador for Christ?

48
On Guard

Guard your heart above all else, for it
determines the course of your life.
PROVERBS 4:23

Many people are captivated by England's Crown Jewels. They are part of the royal collection and are one of the things that tourists flock to see in London. The stars of the Crown Jewel display are the crowns, swords, scepters, rings, and robes used in the coronations of past kings and queens. The Crown Jewels are a reminder of the monarchy's royalty and wealth. So, as you might expect, they are under armed guard in the Jewel House in the Tower of London. Men nicknamed Beefeaters guard the tower and the jewels.

People guard things that are valuable to them. Bankers keep their money in vaults. The wealthy keep their jewels in home safes or in special safe-deposit boxes at the bank. Museums have security guards and a security system with cameras that track every move. Some homeowners have video surveillance and security systems for their houses. Your parents probably keep the money they are saving for a new car or a vacation in the bank. You may even have your own

bank account to keep your money safe. People want to guard what's valuable to them.

What about your heart? Do you guard it? This heart is not the organ that pumps blood through your body. It is a spiritual part of you. It is the source of your thoughts, words, and actions. The Bible says to guard your spiritual heart, because everything flows from it. It determines who you are and what you will be.

How can you guard your heart? By filling it with things that are true, honorable, right, pure, lovely, and admirable (see Philippians 4:8). That might mean not listening to your best friend's favorite music because the songs have lyrics that aren't pure or admirable. It might mean turning off a television show because the main character says things that aren't honorable or lovely. Look for replacements for those things by finding music, shows, books, and activities that encourage positive values and faith in God.

When you guard your heart, the things that flow out of it will be things that please God and help you to be more like Jesus.

Draw a heart on a piece of paper. In the heart, write ten things you want to fill your heart with. You can include the words from Philippians 4:8, list Bible passages you'd like to memorize, or write worship songs that help you think about God. Share the heart you've drawn with your family or a close friend. You can explain what it means to guard your heart.

49
One Way

Jesus told him, "I am the way, the truth, and the life.
No one can come to the Father except through me."

JOHN 14:6

Picture yourself at a state park where there is a cascading waterfall at the outer edge. You'd like to see it, so you look on the map and notice there's a trail that leads right to it. But the trail is rugged and requires climbing up rocks and crossing a stream using a very narrow bridge. The map shows another trail, which looks much easier, that goes near the waterfall. You decide to take the second trail and figure that you'll be able to see the waterfall from where it ends.

You start down the second trail. The path is wide and easy to follow. There's no climbing, so you quickly reach the end of the trail. You look around, expecting to find the waterfall, but you don't see it. You can hear the sound of water in the distance, so you know the waterfall is there. You are at the end of your trail, but you aren't at all where you wanted to be.

That's how it is with getting to heaven. People want to go to heaven. Jesus says that he is the way to heaven and no one gets there without him. But

people ignore what Jesus says in John 14:6. They try to get to heaven by following the Ten Commandments and obeying the laws of their country. They believe doing those things will make them good enough to go to heaven. But that's not how we get to heaven. Isaiah 64:6 says, "We are all infected and impure with sin. When we display our righteous deeds, they are nothing but filthy rags." Without Jesus, our good behavior isn't worth anything.

Some people try to do good works to earn their way to heaven. They give money in the offering, they give food to the poor, and they volunteer in the community. These are good things, but they don't buy a ticket to heaven. Ephesians 2:8-9 says, "God saved you by his grace when you believed. And you can't take credit for this; it is a gift from God. Salvation is not a reward for the good things we have done, so none of us can boast about it." No matter how many good things you may do, you won't get to heaven unless you have asked Jesus to forgive your sins.

Heaven is a free gift. We don't deserve it. We can't earn it. Jesus is the only way to heaven. And that's good news for all of us.

Think of one person who needs to hear today's verse. Share it with him or her. Write down the name of the person you shared it with and what happened. Remember to pray for that person to accept the gift of salvation.

50
Be an Example

Don't let anyone think less of you because you are young.
Be an example to all believers in what you say, in the
way you live, in your love, your faith, and your purity.

1 TIMOTHY 4:12

The apostle Paul wrote today's verse to Timothy, a young pastor. He didn't want Timothy to be discouraged by those who thought he was too young to lead a church. Paul told Timothy to be an example in what he said and did.

Sometimes people today look down on young people. It's true that some teens break rules, wreck other people's property, bully kids, and drive wildly. But there are also teens who are involved in raising money for the homeless, going on short-term mission trips, being tutors and role models for younger students, and doing yard work for the elderly. These young people are making a difference in their corner of the world.

Just as Paul wrote to Timothy, God wants you to be an example too. You can set the standard high for those around you in the words you say, in the way you live, in your love for others, in your relationship with

God, and in the way you participate in good things. How can you do that? When others start gossiping or cutting others down, you can change the subject to something that is positive and uplifting. When class-mates are fighting with or bullying other students, you can be the one to step up with a smile and a kind word. When other kids are talking about a movie they saw that shows bad values, you can turn the talk to a movie that has good values.

Being young isn't a hindrance in serving God. You can use your youthful energy and enthusiasm to shine brightly in your corner of the world at school, home-school events, sports, clubs, tumbling class, music lessons, and home.

Can you think of a time when others didn't take you seriously because you were young? Don't let it hold you back. Find one way to be an example to others each day this week.

51
Created for a Purpose

We are God's masterpiece. He has created us anew in Christ Jesus, so we can do the good things he planned for us long ago.

EPHESIANS 2:10

The *Jetsons* was a family cartoon that was first on television in 1962. The show, set in the future, featured George Jetson; his wife, Jane; their daughter, Judy; their son, Elroy; and the family's dog, Astro, as they went about life in their space-age home and traveled in a flying car. There was even a robot maid, Rosie, to do the housework. At that time, a robot doing work seemed like something far in the future, but now that time is here. Recently a news article listed several jobs where humans might be replaced by robots. Those jobs included counting out pills and distributing them at a pharmacy, reviewing a legal document, driving a car, cleaning a space station, being a soldier in combat, babysitting and entertaining kids, and rescuing victims who are trapped after an earthquake or tornado. These robots were created with a specific purpose in mind, and their creators gave them what they needed for the job they were meant to do.

You aren't like those robots, because you can think and reason. But just as robots were created to do a job, God created you for a specific purpose. There is something he wants you to do with your life. The psalmist said, "You saw me before I was born. Every day of my life was recorded in your book. Every moment was laid out before a single day had passed. How precious are your thoughts about me, O God. They cannot be numbered!" (Psalm 139:16-17). You should never feel as if you, or any other person, were an accident. God doesn't make mistakes. He has a purpose for each person.

God calls you his masterpiece. Because you are his princess, you are able to fulfill the purpose he planned for you before you were born. As you follow God daily, you'll discover that purpose. It's a plan only you can fulfill. So don't hesitate, and don't be a spectator in life. Step out and follow the path God shows you. You can be confident that you have been created for a purpose and for making a difference in your world.

Read Psalm 139. Jot down the things the psalmist says God did for him. How do these promises apply to you personally? Thank God that they are true for you, too.

52
Listen Up

Understand this, my dear brothers and sisters: You must all be quick to listen, slow to speak, and slow to get angry.

JAMES 1:19

The African elephant is the largest kind of elephant. Its ears are one-sixth the size of its body, so it has the largest ears of any animal. Can you imagine how large your ears would be if they were one-sixth of your body size? Your ears would hang from your head to your upper arm! The elephant's large ears funnel sound into its ear canal, and one elephant can hear another elephant up to five miles away!

You spend 70 to 80 percent of your awake time communicating. Of that time, you spend about 45 percent of it listening. So how's your listening? You probably can hear what a parent or teacher says, but how well do you actually listen?

Many people don't have good listening skills. One reason is because we talk at a rate of about 125 words a minute, but our brains can process things at a much faster rate. So you might find yourself thinking about something different, or daydreaming, while a friend is telling you about the argument she had with her mom the other night. Or you might be thinking about how you are going to spend the afternoon while your pastor is preaching the morning sermon.

A test showed that after listening to a 10-minute oral presentation, the average person heard, understood, or remembered only about half of it. Just 48 hours later, the listeners had forgotten half of what they did hear and understand. What that means is that you may remember only 25 percent of your pastor's sermon, your teacher's talk about the battles of the Civil War, or the job your mom wants you to do on the weekend.

Can you see the problem with this? You might miss important information. So the next time someone is talking, focus on what he or she is saying. Listen for key points and even jot them down if you need to. And when your mind starts to wander, summarize to yourself what the person has already said.

God wants you to be swift to listen and slow to speak. He also wants you to listen to what he has to say to you. That might mean listening more carefully to your pastor or Sunday school teacher, but it might also mean reading the Bible and paying attention to what God wants to teach you.

Use your Bible concordance or Biblegateway.com to look up the words *hear* or *listen*. Jot down what the Bible verses say to you about listening.

53
When Things Are Shaking

God is our refuge and strength, always ready to help in times of trouble. So we will not fear when earthquakes come and the mountains crumble into the sea.

PSALM 46:1-2

Have you ever felt an earthquake? Maybe you felt only a minor tremor, or perhaps it was an earthquake that caused damage. The strength of an earthquake is measured in magnitudes, with 10 as the highest. At magnitude 5.5 to 6.0, there is damage to structures and buildings. Earthquakes with a magnitude of 8.0 and greater can destroy a whole community.

In 1960, Chile experienced an earthquake that was a magnitude of 9.5. Thousands of people were killed. Not only that, it also triggered a tsunami that killed people in Japan, the Philippines, and Hawaii. More recently, in 2010, an earthquake with a magnitude of 7.0 shook Haiti. There were many aftershocks that did additional damage. Over three million people were affected by the earthquake, and many Haitians still live in tent cities—areas where only plastic sheets or tents provide shelter.

If you haven't experienced being shaken by a real

earthquake, maybe there has been a time when it felt as if things in your life were shaking. Maybe your dad got a new job and you had to move to a new city. That meant leaving your friends, school, and church behind. Or maybe the transition from elementary school to middle school was rough. It left you confused and trying to find your way. It could be that you are growing and changing, and it seems as if your emotions are going crazy. One minute you're happy, and the next you're sad or worried.

The good thing is that whether you are shaking from a physical earthquake or you feel as if your life is shaking from changes or hard times, God is ready to help. He doesn't always stop earthquakes or even the consequences of them, but he's always there. He'll be with you and give you peace as you go through times of trouble. Take time to read your Bible more during tough times. Connect with God through prayer, and ask him to help you feel his presence.

The psalmist knew that trouble would come, but he had confidence that God would be with him even if the mountains crumbled into the sea.

Take time today to read Psalm 46 and Psalm 91. Both of them are assurances of God's protection during times of trouble. Even if you aren't facing earthquakes in your life now, these are still good psalms to become familiar with for when those tough times come.

54
Work Hard

*She is energetic and strong, a hard worker. . . . She
extends a helping hand to the poor and opens her
arms to the needy. She has no fear of winter for
her household, for everyone has warm clothes.*
PROVERBS 31:17, 20-21

Proverbs 31 is known for its verses about a wife of
good character. Although it's a long time until you'll
be an adult, the characteristics of the Proverbs 31
woman are ones you can start developing now. Today's
verse says a good woman is "energetic and strong"
and "a hard worker." She's prepared for what's ahead.
The wife of good character isn't a dreary housewife
overwhelmed by all she has to do. She is an energetic
woman with many talents and positive characteristics.
These are characteristics God wants you to develop in
your life as his princess.

Think about your own life. There are things you
have to do each day. You have schoolwork to do. Do
you tackle your homework with energy? Not only
that, but do you go beyond that and make sure you're
prepared for the next school day by reviewing your
work to make sure you understand it and look ahead

to what you'll be discussing? Do you take time to make sure you have your books and supplies ready?

Besides your schoolwork, you're probably expected to help at home by making your own bed and taking your dirty clothes to the washing machine or a hamper. You may be assigned to set the table, feed the dog, or empty the trash, too. How do you do those jobs? Do you do them to the best of your ability with energy and cheerfulness? Do you give a little extra and help your brother or sister complete his or her job, or do you complete a job that's not assigned to you just because it needs to be done? That's the princess way.

What you do today will determine what kind of woman you'll be in the future. If you're energetic and cheerful in your work and prepared for what's ahead, you'll be looking at a brighter tomorrow.

Is there too much homework this week? Do your jobs at home seem boring? Make a point to complete all your work on time and cheerfully this week. Go a step further and do an extra job to help out.

55
Being a Princess with Dignity

She is clothed with strength and dignity, and she laughs without fear of the future. When she speaks, her words are wise, and she gives instructions with kindness.

PROVERBS 31:25-26

If you look up the word *dignity* in the dictionary, it will tell you that dignity is the quality of being worthy of honor or respect. One woman in the Bible who had dignity was Abigail. She was married to Nabal, whose name meant "fool," and he lived up to his name. He was a wealthy man with a large flock of sheep. During the time that David was on the run from King Saul, he and his 600 men camped near where Nabal kept his flock. Instead of stealing the sheep for food, David and his men helped keep thieves away.

At shearing time, Nabal had a big celebration for his men. David asked for food for his men, too, since they'd helped guard the sheep. Nabal not only turned David down but also ridiculed and insulted him. David became angry and said he'd kill all the men in Nabal's household.

Fortunately, Nabal's wife was no fool. She was a woman of dignity. And as today's verse says about the noble woman, Abigail spoke with wisdom and kindness. When she heard what her husband had done, she got busy preparing food for David and his men. She also personally went to meet with him and talked him out of killing Nabal and the other men in his household.

Abigail reacted with strength, dignity, and wisdom in a time of trouble. It's easier to maintain your dignity when things are going well, but how about when they're going wrong? When a friend starts an argument, do you stay calm and in control of your emotions? When a teacher unfairly assigns extra homework, do you accept it without complaint? When you're tired and cranky, do you still show respect to your parents and other family members?

The woman in today's verse is a role model for how to live, deal with various situations, and interact with people. Abigail was also an example of how to have dignity, strength, and wisdom. As God's princess, you can follow her example.

Read the story of Abigail, Nabal, and David in 1 Samuel 25. List the things Abigail did that showed she was a woman of dignity. Can you think of a time when you handled a problem with strength, wisdom, and dignity? Write about it.

56
Beauty That Lasts

Charm is deceptive, and beauty does not last; but a woman who fears the LORD will be greatly praised.
PROVERBS 31:30

There was a show on television where young women competed to be models. They lived together and were guided by experienced models. As the weeks passed, there was competition among the contestants to look the most beautiful and to present themselves and their outfits in the best way so they'd appear to be the most likely to succeed as a professional model.

There was a lot of drama among the contestants as they felt the pressure to be the best. Relationships that were formed at the beginning of the competition started to crumble. Because they desired to be the best, the contestants pushed themselves to their limits and became more competitive as the show got closer to choosing a winner.

A lot of people want to impress others by having the perfect body or a beautiful face. They spend their time and money trying to look pretty. God gave you the looks you have, so it's certainly not wrong to care about your appearance or to take care of yourself.

After all, you're a princess of the heavenly King, so be the best princess you can be. But use your looks to honor God, not to hurt others or to get your own way.

Although there's so much emphasis in our culture on being beautiful, inner beauty is much more important than outward beauty. Outward beauty doesn't last. Looks change. People age. But inner beauty grows and increases as you grow closer to Jesus and become more like him. Constantly worrying about your hairstyle or outfit, or wishing you looked more like the popular girls, drains the energy you can use to excel at being who God made you to be. Others are trying to fit in, but God calls you to stand out.

Focus your thoughts and your heart on being beautiful to God. When others see your looks, God sees your inner thoughts and feelings. He knows your desires, your motivations, and your priorities. When you seek to put God first in everything, you'll shine in his eyes. And you'll have beauty that lasts.

Take a good look at yourself in the mirror. Thank God for the special way he made you. Think about your inner beauty. What characteristics show your inner beauty? Are you compassionate? Do you radiate joy? Are you full of kindness? Ask God to help you develop the inner characteristics that make you more like Jesus each day.

57
A Time for Everything

*For everything there is a season, a time for every
activity under heaven. A time to be born and a time
to die. A time to plant and a time to harvest. A
time to kill and a time to heal. A time to tear down
and a time to build up. A time to cry and a time
to laugh. A time to grieve and a time to dance.*

ECCLESIASTES 3:1-4

Do you have a favorite season? Do you prefer
summer when it's hot and you can spend the
day swimming or playing outside until the sun goes
down late? Or maybe you prefer winter when it's cold
and you can go sledding. Maybe spring is your favorite season. Flowers begin to bloom and spread their
color after the darkness of winter. Or perhaps you love
the fall, when leaves turn red, orange, and yellow and
make the trees look like a flaming fire.

God created the times and seasons. He's set the
events of your life in motion—the happy times and
sad, the good times and bad. There will be times in
your life when you rejoice and times when you grieve.
There will be times when you accomplish a lot and
times when you feel less motivated. There will be

times when everything goes your way and days when you feel as if nothing will go right. Life constantly changes. That's the way it's always been. The good thing is that God is in control, and he will be with you every day.

You can't always control the things that happen in your life, but you can determine that you'll have a good attitude during both the good and bad times. You can let the things that happen draw you closer to God and make you more like Jesus rather than let life's circumstances make you either bitter or proud. And in all of it you can decide to obey God and follow his leading no matter what is happening.

God knows what each season will bring you in your life, and he works through the events in ways you can't always see. The important thing is to trust him and allow him to use life's events to guide you and to accomplish his will.

Read Ecclesiastes 3 about the changing seasons of life. Then jot down a list of things that don't change. You might include God's Word (the answers you get from the Bible), the Holy Spirit guiding you, and God's love. What else can go on your list?

58
Fill Up

Let the message about Christ, in all its richness,
fill your lives. Teach and counsel each other with
all the wisdom he gives. Sing psalms and hymns
and spiritual songs to God with thankful hearts.

COLOSSIANS 3:16

What do you fill your life with? Some people fill their lives with sports. They watch the games, memorize the statistics, follow the players' careers, and even collect sports trading cards. Others fill their lives with a certain kind of music. They listen to it, talk about the performers, memorize lyrics, and buy the newest CDs. There are many things people fill their lives with—after-school clubs, friends, music lessons, sports teams, and even schoolwork.

God wants you to fill your life with his Word. The message of Jesus as Savior for the world should be on your mind. It should fill your thoughts and affect your actions. How can you fill your life with the message of Jesus? By taking time each day to read God's Word. The whole Bible points to Jesus. After Adam and Eve sinned, God promised to send a Redeemer. People looked forward to a coming Savior. The Gospels

(Matthew, Mark, Luke, and John) tell the story of Jesus' life on earth, his death, and his resurrection. The book of Acts tells of Jesus' return to heaven and the beginning of his church on the earth. The Epistles (Romans through Jude) give information about how to live as a Christian. The book of Revelation tells about the things that lead up to Jesus' return to the earth, about heaven, and about the final battle between Jesus and Satan.

Learning God's Word is an exciting journey. You can read the Bible in any order. Each part of it has something new for you. Looking for exciting stories? Read Genesis, Judges, and Mark. Want something to encourage you? Read the book of Psalms. Need some wisdom? Read Proverbs. Want to learn more about how to live the Christian life? Read James or Philippians. Or you can read about a certain Bible character or a topic like peace or forgiveness.

Fill your life with God's Word each day. Jump in and start your journey through the Bible today.

Start a Bible-reading journal. Read a chapter from the Bible each day. Or read about the life of a Bible character. Write down the main idea of the chapter or story and how it applies to you. Not sure where to start? Try John or Philippians. Or read about Rebekah in Genesis 24 or Deborah in Judges 4.

59
The Night Sky

When I look at the night sky and see the work of your fingers—the moon and the stars you set in place—what are mere mortals that you should think about them, human beings that you should care for them?

PSALM 8:3-4

Have you ever gone out at night and gazed up at a sky filled with stars? They seem far away and majestic. If you looked closely, you may have been able to pick out some of the constellations. Constellations are groups of stars that make a picture in the sky. They are named after animals, mythological characters, people, or objects. Constellations are located in a certain section of the night sky. You can see different constellations as the earth turns and at different times during different seasons of the year. Of course, if you lived on the equator, you'd actually be able to see all the constellations during the year. But if you lived at the North or South Pole, you'd only be able to see the ones right above you.

Perhaps David was out with his sheep when he gazed into the night sky filled with its bright points of light and was filled with awe and wonder. Perhaps the moon was full—or maybe just a crescent—far above David. The moon and stars were a silent witness to God's power. David wondered why a God great enough to create the stars and moon would care about people.

Since David's time, man has walked on the moon, rockets have been sent into space, and more has been discovered about the moon and stars. But we still gaze at the night sky in awe. The stars still point to a mighty creator. And best of all, that Creator knows you personally. He cares about you.

Think about it—the same God who created the moon and stars cares about what kind of day you are having. He wants you to spend time with him and know him personally. He watches over you day and night, every day of your life.

Go outside and gaze at the night sky the next time it's filled with stars. Read Psalm 8 and Psalm 19. Then write your own psalm about God. It doesn't matter if it sounds perfect as long as it's from your heart to God.

60
I Can Be Content

I know how to live on almost nothing or with everything. I have learned the secret of living in every situation, whether it is with a full stomach or empty, with plenty or little. For I can do everything through Christ, who gives me strength.

PHILIPPIANS 4:12-13

In the 1960s there was a television show called *Gilligan's Island*. It followed the adventures of seven people who were on the SS *Minnow* when it was shipwrecked on a deserted island. The show was about their humorous attempts at survival, their conflicts because of the characters' very different personalities, and their attempts to get back to civilization, most of which were messed up by Gilligan. Despite their difficulties, the castaways made the best of their situation on the island.

Gilligan's Island was merely a comedy, but the apostle Paul faced real problems as he preached the gospel. He was treated badly by those who didn't believe in Jesus. He was beaten, whipped, stoned, and imprisoned for preaching the gospel. Like Gilligan, he was even shipwrecked.

Despite all of this, Paul was content. He said he could live in every situation. What was his secret to being at peace no matter what his situation was like? Paul said, "I can do everything through Christ, who gives me strength" (Philippians 4:13).

Sometimes this verse is used as a "good-luck charm." People quote the verse to say they can win a ball game or pass a test with Christ's help. While God certainly does help Christians when they ask him, this verse goes hand in hand with the previous one about learning to be content in every situation.

This means that when you face hard times, you can face them with Jesus' help. When you are going through a trial, you can have hope through God's strength. God is with you no matter what happens in your life.

Philippians 4:13 doesn't promise that you'll win every game or pass every test. But it does say that Jesus' strength allows you to face life's circumstances with confidence. And that's a special promise for God's princesses.

It's easier to be content when you are remembering to be thankful for the good things in your life rather than dwelling on the hard times. Can you list ten things you are thankful for? Add things to the list as you think of them this week.

61

Love As Jesus Loved

*[Jesus said,] "I am giving you a new commandment:
Love each other. Just as I have loved you, you should
love each other. Your love for one another will
prove to the world that you are my disciples."*

JOHN 13:34-35

One day a boy was given a 12-inch board. His father
told him to use the board as a template to mark
and cut more lumber into 12-inch pieces. The boy
used the original board to measure and cut the second
board. But instead of using the original board to cut
the remaining boards, he used the board he'd just cut.
As he worked, he continued using the most recently
cut board to measure each new board and cut the pile
of lumber. When his father took the board the boy
had cut last and measured it with the first, there was
an inch difference! The man told his son that when
sawing, you should always measure with the original
piece of wood or with the same ruler. That was the
only way to be sure all the pieces would be the same
size as the original.

Jesus gave his disciples a command. They were
to love each other. It would be a sign to the world that

they were Christians. Jesus told them not to just love each other but to love each other the same way he loved them. The disciples could measure their love for each other according to the way Jesus loved them.

Jesus' love was unconditional. He didn't love his disciples less if they made mistakes. He didn't love them according to how much they loved him. He didn't base his love on how well they served him. He loved them no matter what. His love was perfect.

Jesus understands that you can't love others with a perfect love like his, but he wants you to love them through his strength. He wants you to model your love for other Christians after his love. Some people are harder to love than others. You may not feel warm and fuzzy toward them, but you can still have Jesus' love for them.

Jesus told his disciples that their love for one another would show the world they were his followers. What does your love for other Christians show the world?

Ask God to give you his love for other Christians, even those who are hard to love. How will this change the way you act toward them?

62

Standing Apart for God

I plead with you to give your bodies to God because of all he has done for you. Let them be a living and holy sacrifice—the kind he will find acceptable. This is truly the way to worship him. Don't copy the behavior and customs of this world, but let God transform you into a new person by changing the way you think. Then you will learn to know God's will for you, which is good and pleasing and perfect.

ROMANS 12:1-2

For most young princesses, fitting in is important. One test showed this. Ten students were in a classroom. In the front of the room was a chart with three lines, all with different lengths. The students were instructed to raise their hands when the teacher pointed to the longest line. This was done in several classrooms.

In each group, nine of the ten students were secretly instructed to raise their hands when the teacher pointed to the second longest line. But one student wasn't told that. So when the nine students all raised their hands for the second longest line, the lone student had a decision to make. Should the student go along with them even though they were wrong, or should he or she be the lone person not to raise a hand? The one student would glance around at all the raised hands and, 75 percent of the time, would reluctantly raise his or her hand to avoid being left out.

Peer pressure and the desire not to be different caused the one student in each group to choose a wrong answer. The same is often true in life. You don't want to be different, so you watch a movie with friends even though it makes you uncomfortable. You force yourself to laugh at jokes that are more rude than funny. Maybe you ignore another girl because everyone else is ignoring her, even though you think you should make her feel welcome.

Fitting in is the easy choice, but God calls his princesses to stand out. Today's verse says not to act the way the world does, but to let God transform you into a new person—one who stands apart for God. When you do this, God will help you find the things he wants you to do with your life.

It may be hard standing on your own for God right now, but in the long run it will pay off in having the peace and joy that come from seeking to follow God.

What are some areas in which girls try to fit in? What things do they do to try to be like everyone else? List three ways you can stand apart for God, and ask him to help you be more concerned about being set apart for him than about blending in.

63
Putting Others First

Don't be selfish; don't try to impress others.
Be humble, thinking of others as better than
yourselves. Don't look out only for your own
interests, but take an interest in others, too.

PHILIPPIANS 2:3-4

Have you heard that the way to spell JOY is Jesus-Others-Yourself? That means you have real joy when you put Jesus first, others second, and yourself last. It's more than just a cute acrostic. It's true!

In today's verses Paul told the Philippian believers how to have unity and how to care for one another. The same is true for believers today. Being part of the body of Christ is an honor. Believers are all brothers and sisters in Christ. And it's important that they have the unity that comes from being in the family of God.

One of the biggest hindrances to unity is wanting your own way. If everyone tries to get her way or to have her needs met first, there is no unity. God wants his princesses to do things out of love for one another, not out of selfishness. This doesn't mean that you and your interests aren't important. It means that to truly live the way God wants you to means putting others first.

What happens when all Christians try to do that? They listen to one another. They share their needs. They ask how they can help others. They look beyond their own points of view to see another person's point of view. They find a way to work together. They look at what needs to be done, not at what they need. They look for the best way to do it, not at their own preference for how to do it.

Sadly, many Christians forget to do this. When that happens, people are at odds with one another. Friendships break up, and sometimes churches even divide over things that don't really matter, like the color of the new carpet or the exact type of Bible that is used.

As God's princess you have a chance to do things God's way and put other people's needs ahead of your own. You have the chance to set the example in putting Jesus first, others second, and yourself last. That is the real way to have joy.

Use a poster board and markers or felt and puff paints to make a poster that says

Jesus
Others
Yourself

Hang it where you will see it every day.

64
Your Body Is His Temple

*Don't you realize that your body is the temple
of the Holy Spirit, who lives in you and was
given to you by God? You do not belong to
yourself, for God bought you with a high price.
So you must honor God with your body.*

1 CORINTHIANS 6:19-20

What kind of church do you go to? Is it white with a cross on top? Is it a large brick building? It may have a fellowship hall where meals are served or a gym where games take place. Your church plays an important part in your life. You may go just for worship services, or there may be other activities that take place there during the week.

In Bible times people had the Temple to go to. It was an important place. Solomon, King David's son, built the Temple as a place to put the Ark of the Covenant, which held the Ten Commandments. David had wanted to build the Temple, but God told him, "You must not build a Temple to honor my name, for you are a warrior and have shed much blood" (1 Chronicles 28:3). The magnificent Temple in Jerusalem had both an outside part for the people, an

inside part where the priests served, and an even holier place where God dwelled.

The Temple was a holy place where God dwelled among his people. It was set apart for him. Your body is the temple of God's Holy Spirit, and he asks you to keep yourself clean and pure for him. By valuing your body, you are honoring God, who created you and redeemed you.

Paul wrote to the church at Corinth to tell them that they were God's temple and that the Holy Spirit lived in them. As a princess of God, you have the same promise that the Holy Spirit dwells in you. He helps you live in a way that honors God. He gives you comfort and courage. He gives you strength and power to have the victory over sin.

Look online or in a Bible dictionary to find a picture of Solomon's Temple. Can you locate the Holy Place? You may want to make a sketch of it to remind you that God's Spirit dwells in you just as God dwelled among his people in the Temple. What things can you do to value your body—his temple?

65
God Is Faithful

The faithful love of the LORD never ends! His mercies never cease. Great is his faithfulness; his mercies begin afresh each morning.

LAMENTATIONS 3:22-23

Have you ever sung the hymn "Great Is Thy Faithfulness"? If you have, you are probably familiar with today's verses, because Thomas Chisholm wrote the hymn based on Lamentations 3:22-23.

Born in Kentucky in 1866, Thomas was educated in a small country school, and at the age of 16 he became the school's teacher. Thomas came to know Jesus at the age of 27. He was a pastor for a while, but he was often in poor health.

Thomas always liked to write, and he wrote 1,200 poems. Eight hundred of his poems were published in Sunday school papers and Christian magazines. Some of those poems became hymns. Thomas wrote "Great Is Thy Faithfulness" as a testimony of God's constant presence through his life and his illnesses.

The prophet Jeremiah was the author of today's verses. Known as the "weeping prophet," Jeremiah was born during a dark time in Judah's history when God's

people weren't listening to God. So he chose Jeremiah to go to the people and tell them to turn back to the Lord. They didn't listen, so God allowed them to be taken captive by another country.

It was during this captivity that Jeremiah penned the words, "I will never forget this awful time, as I grieve over my loss. Yet I still dare to hope when I remember this: The faithful love of the LORD never ends! His mercies never cease. Great is his faithfulness; his mercies begin afresh each morning" (Lamentations 3:20-23).

Even when God's people aren't faithful to him, he loves them and shows compassion toward them. He never tires of being faithful or having mercy on his people. God's faithfulness gave Jeremiah hope. He remembered that he needed to depend on the Lord and trust in him even though outward circumstances looked bleak.

You may have good days and bad days in your faith journey. Some days it's much easier to see God at work than others. But good days or bad, God is faithful, and his faithfulness gives hope. It allows you to know that no matter what happens, God is in control and at work. He has a plan for each thing that happens.

Have a parent help you find the hymn "Great Is Thy Faithfulness" online, and listen to the hymn together. What do today's verses mean for you?

66
A Good Motto

Be on guard. Stand firm in the faith.
Be courageous. Be strong.

1 CORINTHIANS 16:13

If you're part of a group like the Girl Scouts or 4-H, you have a motto to live by. The Girl Scout motto is "Be prepared." The 4-H motto is "To make the best better." These mottoes help Girl Scouts or 4-H members focus on a specific task or character trait.

What would you choose if you were going to choose a motto as God's princess? There are many things in Scripture that would make good mottoes. "Do to others what you would like them to do to you" (see Matthew 7:12). "Seek God first" (see Matthew 6:33). "Trust in the Lord with all your heart" (see Proverbs 3:5). Can you think of more?

Today's verse is like a four-part motto for following God. "Be on guard. Stand firm in the faith. Be courageous. Be strong." These are things the apostle Paul instructed the Christians in Corinth to do, and they are the same things God wants you to do.

The first command is to be on guard. Just as a soldier stands guard against attacks, you can be

131

watchful and vigilant against sin. The more you read your Bible and the more you learn about Jesus, the easier it will be to spot things that are not pleasing to God.

The second part of the verse says to stand firm. God wants you to hold tight to what the Bible says and to your values and beliefs. He wants you to be confident in him and in what he can do. Then nothing can shake your faith.

The last two directions are to be courageous and to be strong. These are the same things God told Joshua in Joshua 1:9: "This is my command—be strong and courageous! Do not be afraid or discouraged. For the LORD your God is with you wherever you go." God promised Joshua that he would be with him and lead him. He promises you the same thing. You aren't leading the Israelites into a new land like Joshua was, but you are on a journey to draw closer to God and to live out the plan he has for you. You don't have to have the strength and courage on your own. God will give you his.

What one verse or sentence would you use as your motto for your Christian journey? Write it on a card, and put it where you'll see it. Ask God to help you live out your motto this week.

67

Be Prepared

*If someone asks about your hope as a
believer, always be ready to explain it.*

1 PETER 3:15

The previous devotion mentioned that the Girl Scout motto is "Be prepared." This means a Girl Scout is willing to help and knows what to do. Today's verse is similar to the Girl Scout motto. The apostle Peter says Christians need to always be ready, or prepared, but in this case he means we should always be ready to tell others about the hope we have.

You, as God's princess, know the source of hope. God's own Son, Jesus, came to earth to provide salvation to all who believe in him and have accepted his gift of forgiveness. When you asked Jesus to be your Savior, you became a princess of the heavenly King, which means you'll also spend eternity in heaven with him. Knowing this changes your life and gives you purpose.

When you're living for Jesus, others notice. They see how you treat others and how you're always filled with joy. They may want that for themselves. God wants you to be ready to tell your friends and classmates about the difference Jesus makes in your life. You don't have to

have all the answers. You don't have to know everything about the Bible. You don't have to understand everything about God. No one does. But God wants you to be able to share how Jesus made a difference in your life.

What would you say if a friend asked you why you handle the problems in your life in a calm way? What if she asked you why you seem happy all the time? What if she asked you why you don't watch some of the movies other girls your age do?

One way to answer these questions is by sharing how God sent his Son Jesus to die for our sins. One verse that explains it is John 3:16. "This is how God loved the world: He gave his one and only Son, so that everyone who believes in him will not perish but have eternal life." Another good verse to share with someone who wants to learn about Jesus is Romans 6:23: "The wages of sin is death, but the free gift of God is eternal life through Christ Jesus our Lord."

Using those verses, you can share how God sent his Son Jesus to the earth, how Jesus lived a sinless life so that he could die to pay the penalty for sin, and how he didn't stay dead but rose from the grave and is now with God in heaven. Only by believing in him can someone have the same hope you have—the hope of salvation and an eternity in heaven.

What would you say if someone asked you what makes the difference in your life? Jot down some things you might say.

68
Planting Seeds

[The Lord said,] "The rain and snow come down from the heavens and stay on the ground to water the earth. They cause the grain to grow, producing seed for the farmer and bread for the hungry. It is the same with my word. I send it out, and it always produces fruit. It will accomplish all I want it to, and it will prosper everywhere I send it."

ISAIAH 55:10-11

A lack of rain is called a drought. Everything dries up and turns brown. One time this happened was the "Dust Bowl" period in the 1930s. The Dust Bowl was one of the most destructive droughts in history. A lack of rain, along with poor soil management, caused the top layers of soil in the Great Plains to turn to dust. Enormous dust storms called "black rollers" or "black blizzards" occurred. Some of the dust clouds traveled as far as the East Coast. Many farmers had to move.

What does a drought have to do with the Bible? Today's verse says that just as snow and rain water the earth and cause grain to grow, God's Word goes out and will produce fruit. There is no drought when it comes to the Bible. God's Word accomplishes what it is meant to do. This does not mean that every time someone hears the Bible, he or she will believe in Jesus or accept the Bible's teaching, but God's Word will accomplish what God plans for it to do.

When you share a verse of Scripture with someone, you are planting a seed in that person's heart. That seed may grow, or it may not. Or it may grow over time as another person waters it by sharing more of God's message with the person. Planting and watering are both important, but it's really God who does the work in making the seed of truth grow in someone's heart. The apostle Paul told the church at Corinth, "It's not important who does the planting, or who does the watering. What's important is that God makes the seed grow. The one who plants and the one who waters work together with the same purpose. And both will be rewarded for their own hard work" (1 Corinthians 3:7-8).

Is there someone near you today who needs a seed of truth planted in his or her heart? Perhaps there's a student who seems like she would never be interested in God. Or there's a neighbor girl who has so much going for her she doesn't seem to need God. Plant the seed anyway. God's Word is powerful, and you never know who might need to hear the gospel message today.

List three people who may need to hear God's Word. How can you plant that seed in their hearts? Ask God to give you wisdom about how to do that.

69
A True Friend

*A friend is always loyal, and a brother
is born to help in time of need.*

PROVERBS 17:17

One day a conversation took place between God
and Satan. It was about a man named Job. The
Bible tells us that Job was blameless. He lived for God
and tried hard not to sin (see Job 1:1).

God said to Satan, "Have you noticed my servant
Job? He is the finest man in all the earth. He is blameless—a man of complete integrity. He fears God and
stays away from evil" (Job 1:8).

Satan said that Job feared God only because God
had given him so much. Satan told God, "You have
always put a wall of protection around him and his
home and his property. You have made him prosper in
everything he does. Look how rich he is!" (Job 1:10).

God gave Satan permission to test Job. The book
of Job tells how Job lost all his possessions, servants,
animals, and even sons and daughters. Yet he
remained faithful to God.

Job had three friends who came to talk to him.
They wanted to grieve with him. But they felt that his

troubles were sent by God to punish Job for bad things he had done. They accused him of doing wrong. Job's friends would have been much better friends if they had just been there for him rather than assumed bad things about him.

Today's verse says that a friend is always loyal. Another version says, "A friend loves at all times" (NIV). Job's friends might have thought they were being loyal and loving, but they weren't doing what Job needed.

When tough times come, you want friends who will stand beside you. Friends who will point your thoughts toward God but not assume that your problems are because of sin. As they did to Job, bad things can happen to good people.

It's also important for you to be a loyal and loving friend for others around you. See a friend who is discouraged? Be an encourager. See a friend struggling? Be a helper. See a friend who's hurting? Be a compassionate listener.

As God's princess you can be the friend others need. You have God's love and his message to share with others. How can you be a friend who loves at all times? List three ways you will try to be that kind of friend.

70

Put God First

Seek the Kingdom of God above all else, and live righteously, and he will give you everything you need.

MATTHEW 6:33

George Müller ran an orphanage in Bristol, England, in the 1800s. George is best known for his faith. One morning the 300 orphans who lived in the orphanage woke up for breakfast, but there was no food and no money to buy any. George told the house-mother to take the children to the dining room. When everyone was seated, George thanked God for the food and waited.

Soon there was a knock at the door. It was a baker. He said he knew the orphanage would need bread that day, so he got up early and baked lots of bread. A while later there was another knock at the door. It was the milkman. At that time milk was delivered to people using a cart and horses. The man's cart had broken down. He knew that by the time he fixed the cart, the milk would have gone sour. So he gave the orphanage ten large cans of milk.

Today's verse says if you seek God first and live righteously, God will give you what you need. George

Müller lived that verse out. He put God first in his life, and he trusted the Lord to supply the things he needed in order to keep the children healthy and fed. God provided for their needs.

The same promise is true for you today. God wants you to seek him first. How can you do that? By reading his Word and trying to live it out in your daily life. By asking him to speak to your heart through the Bible and through your pastor's sermon or the Sunday school lesson. By obeying God when he prompts you to do something.

When you put God first by giving some of your money in the offering, sharing a Bible verse with a friend, reaching out to someone who is lonely, cheerfully doing your chores at home, and spending time with God each day, he will bless your life. You might not have the latest game system or electronic gadgets. You might not have the latest styles or most expensive brand of gym shoes, but you'll have God's approval, and that is far better.

In what ways can you seek to put God first this week? How can you put him first in your schoolwork? In time spent with your family? In your chores? In your free-time activities? Write down some ideas, and choose one to do each day.

71

Jesus Is the Lighthouse

*Jesus spoke to the people once more and said,
"I am the light of the world. If you follow me,
you won't have to walk in darkness, because
you will have the light that leads to life."*

JOHN 8:12

Shipping was important in early American life. Ships and boats were how people and goods were transported. But shipping could be dangerous. There were storms, sandbars, shallow water, and rocky coastlines. If a ship was wrecked, people and cargo would be lost. Before lighthouses were built to guide ships, lanterns or fires were used. But each region used a different system of where and how the lanterns or fires would be lit, and that got confusing. So lighthouses were built.

The most important job of a lighthouse is to shine a bright light at night. Sometimes the light shows where the harbor is. Other times it helps the ship move around hazards. At night a sailor can look at a light and know which lighthouse it is by its characteristics. For instance, the sailor might recognize the lighthouse because the light flashes every ten seconds.

Lighthouses were the best way to keep ships safe at night and during storms.

Just as a lighthouse guides ships to safety and helps them steer around danger, Jesus is the light that guides people to salvation and provides spiritual direction. God sent Jesus into a world dark with sin in order to be the light. Jesus paid the price for sin so that salvation could be available to anyone who believes. Maybe some of your friends and the people around you are adrift in a sea of spiritual darkness. Maybe they don't know where to find peace and forgiveness.

As God's princess, you can reflect Jesus' light to the world. Jesus lights your life with love each day. He helps you stand out in the dark world. Through the goodness and love that fill your life, others can be drawn to the Savior.

Have you ever seen a lighthouse? What was it like? If you haven't, maybe that is something you could visit on your next family vacation. Find out the history of the lighthouse and how the lighthouse keeper would keep the light shining bright. If you can't visit a lighthouse, ask a parent to help you find a website that shows how a lighthouse works. How is a lighthouse like Jesus' work in drawing others to himself?

72
Got Peace?

*You will keep in perfect peace all who trust in
you, all whose thoughts are fixed on you!*

ISAIAH 26:3

What are you thinking about right now? Maybe
what happened at school today is on your
mind, or perhaps you're thinking of a fun activity
that is coming up. You might be having a problem
with a friend, and you can't stop thinking about it. Or
perhaps a homework assignment you just can't figure
out is on your mind.

The thoughts that fill your mind affect your
mood. If you doubt that, think about the last time you
had an argument with someone. Afterward it probably
filled your mind and made you feel sad or angry. Think
about a time when something really good happened,
like getting a surprise birthday present or earning an
A on a big project. Your thoughts were probably happy,
and your mood was upbeat.

God gives a great promise in today's verse. He
promises perfect peace. That doesn't mean bad things
won't bother you or fill your thoughts. It means you'll
have an inner calmness or quiet and know that all

is well because you belong to God, even when bad things happen.

Because you are God's princess, your heart belongs to him, and you can trust in him. You have the confidence that God is strong and faithful and that he is in control of all things.

The psalmist David was someone who knew the truth of keeping his mind focused on God and of feeling real peace because of it. He wrote, "Even when I walk through the darkest valley, I will not be afraid, for you are close beside me. Your rod and your staff protect and comfort me" (Psalm 23:4). David knew the secret of having peace in the midst of problems. He kept his mind focused on God's ability to take care of everything.

What does all this talk of peace have to do with you? It's easy. If your heart and your mind are focused on God, his peace will take you through times when others around you aren't feeling peace. When they are questioning why things happen, you'll be at peace because you'll know that God has a plan for everything that happens in your life.

The Bible has a lot to say about peace. Use your Bible to look up three of the verses listed below, and read them. Write down what they have to say to you.

Psalm 29:11   John 16:33
Psalm 119:165   Romans 15:13
John 14:27   Philippians 4:6-7

73
Keep Going

*My dear brothers and sisters, be strong and immovable.
Always work enthusiastically for the Lord, for you
know that nothing you do for the Lord is ever useless.*

1 CORINTHIANS 15:58

Tug-of-war is a game that tests the strength of
two teams as they face off against each other.
You might have played this game at recess or in PE.
Some people take the game very seriously. At one
time tug-of-war was a royal sport played in Egypt and
China. It was an Olympic game from 1900 to 1920.
Today, it is still part of some important competitions
like the World Games and the Scottish Highland
Games and is played in almost every country.

The official rules for tug-of-war call for two teams
of eight people, one team on each end of a rope. The
center mark of the rope is directly above a line on the
ground. Each team attempts to pull the other team
across that line. In order to win the competition, the
players must continue pulling and not let up for even
a moment, or they will be pulled over the line. The
team with both the most strength and the most perseverance wins.

Showing consistent strength and perseverance is also needed when doing the Lord's work. The apostle Paul encouraged the believers to be strong and immovable while serving God enthusiastically. He knew that it would be easy for them to get tired or discouraged when doing God's work.

Sometimes it may seem like you share the gospel with your friends, invite people to church, and help with missionary projects or community service but never see any results. But the work you do for Jesus is never wasted or useless. That's because success isn't measured by getting a trophy or becoming famous. It's not measured by how many people like you or think you are doing a good job. It's measured by spiritual values—or by how much difference what you do makes for eternity. Maybe only two or three friends attend church because you asked them to. For those friends, your work made a difference.

Keep being faithful. Keep standing firm. Work enthusiastically for God, and leave the results to him.

Keep inviting friends to church. Keep sharing Scripture with your friends. Keep giving book reports about Christian books and history reports about people who believed in God. It may not seem like it's making a difference now, but if you are sincerely doing these things for God, he'll use them to reach others.

74
Be like a Tree

They are like trees planted along the riverbank,
bearing fruit each season. Their leaves never
wither, and they prosper in all they do.

PSALM 1:3

Do you like trees? Maybe you like to climb them, or maybe you sit under their shade on hot summer days. In the fall, it's fun to see leaves on some kinds of trees turn to red, yellow, and orange. Trees that are well planted and strong can live a long time, sometimes thousands of years.

The Olive Tree of Vouves, located on the Greek island of Crete, is one of the world's oldest trees. It's been standing for thousands of years. That means it was already growing when Jesus walked on earth, maybe long before. The apostle Paul might have walked by that tree on one of his missionary journeys. The Olive Tree of Vouves still stands strong and produces olives today.

The psalmist David compares godly people to a tree that is planted by a river and produces fruit. He was thinking of a tree with deep roots that draw moisture from the ground. It stands sturdy through droughts or storms. You are like that tree. Just as the tree has

roots to support it and draw moisture, you have roots of faith in Jesus. He is your Savior, and because of that you can stand strong during life's storms.

A tree like the one David refers to has grown and matured over time. In the same way, you started your faith journey as a sapling, and you've been growing since. And the more you dig into God's Word, learn about him, and do your best to follow him, the more you'll grow and mature, just as the flourishing tree did.

The tree David talks about in Psalm 1 also produces fruit. As a child of God allowing his Spirit to work in you, you can be full of good works, or fruit. How that looks in your life depends on the gifts God has given you for serving him. Perhaps you are an encourager who lifts others up when they are down. Or maybe you are a teacher who helps explain things to others. You might be a supporter who stands behind others and helps them with their tasks. Or you may be a leader who steps out and leads others in doing healthy and useful things.

God wants you to be like a tree that is growing and flourishing and producing fruit. He will help you to grow strong as you grow in your faith.

Go for a walk in your neighborhood or local park. Take a picture of the largest, strongest tree you can find. Ask a parent to help you get a print of the picture. Tape it to your mirror to remind you to be strong and mature like that tree.

75
Take Out the Trash

Search me, O God, and know my heart; test
me and know my anxious thoughts. Point
out anything in me that offends you, and lead
me along the path of everlasting life.

PSALM 139:23-24

You most likely have jobs to do to help out around the house. Your brother, sister, and parents have chores too. It is someone's job to take out the trash. That family member might empty all the wastebaskets into a bigger trash can each day, or he or she might just collect it all once or twice a week, when it's time for the garbage truck to come pick it up. If you forget to take out the kitchen trash, it soon starts to smell. Rotted vegetable peels and rotten potatoes especially smell bad, and that's often a reminder you forgot to do your job.

Just as you get rid of the trash that accumulates in your house, it's important to get rid of the trash that builds up in your life. The psalmist David was aware of that. He asked God to search his heart and thoughts and to point out any wrong thing. That's important to do.

As you go through the day, you may not give a lot of thought to each decision you make, each reaction you have, or each word you say. That's why it's a good idea to take time each night to think about the day. Were there times you felt God speaking to your heart or prompting you to do something? Did you do it? Were there things that you did or said that you knew God didn't want you to do or say? How did you feel afterward? Do you owe someone an apology?

When you start doing this each night, it will make you more aware of what you do during the day. It will help guide your thoughts and actions and help you to consider what God wants you to do in each situation.

Like the psalmist, take inventory of your heart, and ask God to take away any trash.

Volunteer to be the one to collect the trash at your house this week if it's not already your job. Share Psalm 139:23-24 with your family.

76
Increase My Borders

[Jabez] was the one who prayed to the God of Israel, "Oh, that you would bless me and expand my territory! Please be with me in all that I do, and keep me from all trouble and pain!" And God granted him his request.

1 CHRONICLES 4:10

If you were to ask God for something, what would it be? Abijah, Asa, and Joshua requested victory in battle. Solomon asked for wisdom. Abraham, Isaac, and Zechariah all prayed for children for their wives. Hannah asked God for a son. Samson asked God for strength. Moses prayed for water, and Elijah requested a drought.

A little-known Bible character named Jabez prayed that God would bless him and expand his territory, be with him in all he did, and keep him from trouble and pain. Those were all good things to pray for. When Jabez asked God to bless him and expand his territory, he may have been asking God to actually give him more land. But as a princess of the heavenly King, you can ask God to bless you and expand your spiritual territory, or your area of ministry—in other words, increase the number of people you share Jesus with.

151

Right now your territory is the people you see often: your family, your neighborhood friends, other students in your class or homeschool group, people in your Sunday school class, your teammates, or kids taking lessons with you. It might seem that none of those people need you to tell them about Jesus. But even if they have heard about Jesus many times, they may not have accepted him as their Savior yet. If they have, maybe they need an encouraging word or someone to listen to their problems or doubts.

If you are already part of a church ministry that visits in homes and tells people about Jesus or invites them to church, that's great. Or you might be part of a church that has a food pantry or clothing ministry for the poor. That's good too. Sharing your faith and living it out in a practical way is important.

If you feel like you could be doing more to reach others or to make a real difference to those around you, ask God to expand your territory. Then talk to your parents about ways to be more involved. You may want to talk to your church leaders about it too. They may have some suggestions about how you can get more involved in sharing your faith and reaching others in your community.

What's your spiritual territory? How are you reaching out to others? If you aren't, list possible ways you might be able to do that, and then talk to an adult about it.

77
Dig a Little Deeper

Study this Book of Instruction continually.
Meditate on it day and night so you will be
sure to obey everything written in it. Only then
will you prosper and succeed in all you do.

JOSHUA 1:8

Joshua was a leader with a big job ahead. He was in charge of leading the Israelites into their new home after they'd wandered in the wilderness for 40 years. He wasn't in charge of just a few people. He was the leader of two to three million Israelites. Moses had led the Israelites through the wilderness, and now God had called Joshua to finish the work.

God didn't leave Joshua without any guidance, though. He told Joshua to read God's law continually, to think about it, and to obey it. If Joshua would do this, God would give him success in leading the people.

You aren't a leader of millions entering a new land, but these instructions are for you, a princess of God, just as they were for Joshua, the leader of God's people. The good thing is that you have God's complete instruction manual for living as his princess in today's world. Just as you study your math facts or a science chapter for a test, God wants you to study the Bible so you'll know what it has to say to you. You can dig a little deeper into his Word. As you read through it, try to understand each verse. If you don't, ask a parent to help you find a book or website that helps girls your age understand the Bible. Or maybe you and a parent or another adult could do a Bible study together. God didn't tell Joshua to stop with just studying God's laws. He told Joshua to think about God's laws night and day so he'd be sure to obey them. After you read the Bible each day, spend some time thinking about it. During the day, ask yourself how it applies to you. Once you get into the habit of doing this, you'll find yourself focusing more on God throughout the day and on how you can live as his princess.

Challenge a friend or your mom or sister to study the Bible with you. Get a Bible study book at your local Christian bookstore, or choose a book of the Bible to read through a few verses at a time. You might want to keep a journal so you can write down what you read, what it means, and how you can live it out daily.

78
God Guides Your Steps

The LORD directs the steps of the godly.
He delights in every detail of their lives.
PSALM 37:23

In the movie *Monsters University*, Mike is the leader of an unlikely team of monsters who take part in a competition, called the Scare Games, to become the top scarers. The teams face challenges, and one team is eliminated in each competition. One of the challenges is to make it through the library and get the team flag without getting caught by the librarian. Mike guides his team through the library by telling them to do exactly what he does. They copy every move he makes, whether he plans for them to or not.

Just as Mike led his team in the library competition, God is your team leader. He wants to direct your steps so that you walk the path he has for you. When you joined God's team, he already had a plan for your life. He gave you the talents and abilities to embark on this journey he's planned for you. God doesn't want you to just go through life without purpose. He wants you to run joyfully down the specially designed path he has for you.

God has a different plan for each princess, so trying to copy someone else's steps doesn't work. That's why it's important to ask God to direct your own steps each day. When you get up in the morning, ask him to show you what he wants you to do that day. As you walk down the school hallway or get ready to study at home, ask him who he wants you to talk to or encourage. Ask him to guide you when you're with your family and when you're with friends.

When you obey God's Word and listen to his voice, your steps will be sure and straight, and you will be following the plan he has just for you.

Trace your foot on a piece of colored paper. Cut it out and write today's verse on it. Put it somewhere you will see it to be a reminder to let God guide your steps each day.

79
God Hears and Answers

We are confident that [God] hears us whenever
we ask for anything that pleases him. And since we
know he hears us when we make our requests,
we also know that he will give us what we ask for.

1 JOHN 5:14-15

Each year many people make a list of presents they want for Christmas. You may even do that. The list might include new clothes or the latest style of shoes. It might include books written by your favorite author or a new series you want to read. The list might have movies or music on it. And it probably has some of the latest electronic games or gadgets. Once the list is made, it's given to the person in charge of buying the presents in your family.

Sometimes when people pray, it sounds a lot like a Christmas list. "Fix this problem and this problem." "Heal that person and another person." "Give me this and this and this." Today's verses say that God will grant the requests that please him. So if something on your prayer list goes against the Bible, then he's not going to grant that request. Or if it's something God knows won't help you be a better person or have a

stronger faith in him, he is not going to give it to you. But when you ask for things that help you follow him better or honor him, he wants to answer that.

God wants to hear more than just your requests though. He wants to hear your confessions, because when you admit to God the mistakes you made, he forgives them. He also wants to hear your praise. You probably know what praise is because if you've done a good job at something, a parent or teacher has praised you. When you turn your praise to God, you recognize who he is and what he's done, and you express that back to him with love and gratitude.

If you aren't used to including all these things in your prayers, it may seem awkward at first. You might want to read a psalm of praise or thanksgiving (like Psalm 100 or Psalm 145) as part of your prayer time. Even though they're not your words, God knows your heart, and he'll know if the words are sincere.

Keeping a prayer journal can make your prayer life richer. Decorate your journal (a cloth book or simple spiral notebook). Use it to keep track of prayer requests and the answers to those. List things to praise and thank God for. You can even copy some verses from Psalms that reflect how you're feeling.

80

Be an Encourager

*Encourage each other and build each other
up, just as you are already doing.*

1 THESSALONIANS 5:11

"You can do it!" "Good try!" "You're doing a great
job." These are words of encouragement you
might hear spoken to you by a parent, teacher, or
friend. Hearing them probably makes you feel good
inside and inspires you to try harder. Encouragement
is like that.

God's princesses can be great encouragers for
others. You may talk to many different people each
day. God plans for you to make a difference in their
lives. You can have a positive influence on other people
by speaking words that are helpful and uplifting. In
order to be an encourager, you have to be focused on
others. Take your eyes off yourself, and look around for
someone who needs a positive reminder.

How can you encourage others today? An easy
way is with your words. Telling people what they are
doing right or inspiring them not to give up may be just
the boost they need to keep going on a difficult task.

Another way to encourage a friend, fellow

student, or family member is to pitch in and help out with a chore, problem, or project. Sometimes doing a job or an assignment alone seems overwhelming, but when someone steps up and says, "I'll help you," it makes a big difference. Suddenly the task seems possible.

Go a step beyond, and encourage someone by serving him or her. Does your mom look worn out? Do a job for her so she can take a break. Does your brother look stressed? Do something kind for him without letting him see you. Step up and do something for someone else without expecting anything in return.

There are a lot of discouragers in the world. They are the ones who want you to believe you aren't pretty enough, talented enough, or smart enough. They cause you to doubt your abilities or make you think you aren't capable of doing certain things. Don't listen to the discouragers, and don't be one either. Be the kind of person who supports others and rejoices in their successes.

Who have you noticed that needs a word of encouragement? Look around for someone who is struggling with an assignment or a chore. Look for someone who is discouraged. What can you say to make a difference? How can your help encourage him or her?

81

A Winner in God's Eyes

Thank you for making me so wonderfully complex!
Your workmanship is marvelous—how well I know it.
PSALM 139:14

Most schools have a group of "in" girls. Those are the girls that are cute, funny, and stylish. You often see them gathered in a little group in the hall. You might have walked by them and wished you were part of the group because they seem to have it all together—looks, clothes, and personality. Or maybe you're part of that group, but you don't really feel as if you have it all together.

Sometimes it seems as if some girls have more than their share of beauty, personality, and talents. They wear the newest styles and have the latest gadgets. And sometimes that just doesn't seem fair.

The good news is that beauty, an outgoing personality, and talents don't make you a winner in God's eyes. You are already a winner to him because he personally created you the exact way he wanted to. He created you to be a one-of-a-kind princess to serve and worship him. So when you think of yourself as being specially created by the God who created

the whole universe, you'll start to see yourself as
a winner.

Unfortunately, not everyone in life will value your
worth. In fact, some girls can get downright mean with
girls they don't think are as good as they are. They
may ignore them, gossip about them, or start rumors
about them.

Those things can hurt if you are on the receiv-
ing end of them, but they don't change who you are
inside. Surround yourself with friends who value you
for who you are. Don't be sucked in to the comparison
game and judge yourself by how your looks, clothes,
belongings, and even your friends measure up to
theirs. That's not what really matters. Sure, it's okay
to want to look your best and wear nice clothes, but
remember, that's not what gives you your worth. Your
worth comes from God. You don't have to be part of a
certain group to be "in" with God.

Appearances change, clothes become outdated,
and friends grow apart, but you are forever God's
princess, and nothing can change that.

Think about it. How do you judge your worth? Have
you gotten sucked in to the comparison game? Do you
let what others think of you overshadow your worth to
God? Read 1 Peter 3:3-4 in your Bible, and take time to
reflect on your real worth.

82

Using Words for Good

May the words of my mouth and the
meditation of my heart be pleasing to you,
O LORD, my rock and my redeemer.

PSALM 19:14

How many words do you speak per day? Studies have been done to try to figure out how many words a person speaks in a day, but there are some big differences in their findings. One popular study reported that adult women speak as many as 30,000 words a day, while adult men speak only 7,000 words a day. Another study showed that both men and women speak about 16,000 words a day.

Those numbers would vary by a person's personality and the type of job he or she has. A person with a job in teaching or customer service would use more words than a person who works alone. A naturally outgoing person would use more words than a shy person.

The same is true for you. There are lots of times during the day when you are quietly listening to a lesson being taught or doing your schoolwork. There are other times like lunch and recess when you might talk a lot if you're a talkative person, or not so much if you're shy or just like to listen more than talk. Either way, you probably use several thousand words a day.

Words alone have no power, but when you speak them, you give them power. The words you speak can hurt, or they can heal. They can build a person up or tear him or her down. They can pass on the good news of Jesus or spread vicious gossip. They can lie, or they can speak truth.

Imagine the difference your words can make. You can speak 10,000 words a day that are inspirational and encouraging or 10,000 words a day that are meaningless or even harmful. That makes a big difference. One way leaves those around you feeling good about themselves, encouraged to try again, or hopeful and happy. The other way leaves them feeling discouraged, angry, or disappointed.

Which way will you use your words today? Will what you say make someone's life better? Will your words be a blessing to a teacher or a parent? Will they encourage a friend to try harder? Will they make someone's day brighter?

In today's verse the psalmist says, "May the words of my mouth and the meditation of my heart be pleasing to you, O Lord, my rock and my redeemer." Why not pray this same prayer each morning and every time you're tempted to use your words in wrong ways? It will make a big difference in your life and in the lives of those you talk to.

83
Friends

Walk with the wise and become wise;
associate with fools and get in trouble.

PROVERBS 13:20

Your friends are important. They are the ones you laugh with, cry with, share your heart with, and hang out with. They know your likes and dislikes. They know what your favorite movie is and which school subject you enjoy the most. They may be the ones who help you with the math homework you don't understand or coach you on your spelling words.

Your friends play such a significant role in your life that it's crucial to have the right kind of friends. What should you look for in a friend?

A good friend puts others first. Sure, each friend can have a say about what to do when you're together, but a good friend doesn't always demand her own way. She is willing to share in her friends' activities and interests. Shared interests make good memories.

A good friend listens. A good friend lets you share your stories, problems, and ideas rather than dominate the conversation with her own. She should

165

want to hear what you have to say too. Like you, she is learning to take turns talking so no one is left out.

A good friend tells the truth. A true friend doesn't pretend to like something she doesn't really like. She doesn't pretend something's okay if it's not. That doesn't mean hurting a friend's feelings; it means speaking the truth with love.

A good friend shows respect for others. That means showing appreciation for another person's worth or for the person's authority if he or she is a parent, a teacher, or someone who is in charge. A friend who respects others speaks kindly, takes turns, treats others fairly, and puts others' needs ahead of her own.

As you look for people who will be good friends for you, make sure to be a good friend for others. Challenge each other to be the best you can be. Today's verse says, "Walk with the wise and become wise; associate with fools and get in trouble." With the right friend, you can make good choices and be your best together.

What characteristics do you think are most important in a friend? How do you show those to your friends? Write down ways you can do that in the coming week.

84
Follow the Leader

Follow my example, as I follow the example of Christ.
1 Corinthians 11:1 (NIV)

Have you ever played follow the leader? First, a leader is chosen. This person goes to the head of the line, and everyone else lines up behind her. The leader then moves around and does different actions, and the followers have to exactly copy the leader's movements. If someone fails to do what the leader does, she's out of the game. The last one in the game becomes the leader for the next game.

Sometimes you may follow the leader in real life, too. Have you ever repeated something another person said? Have you ever worn a certain kind of clothing because it looked good on a friend or a popular girl? Have you ever joined an activity because someone you admire joined it? Those are ways you might follow the leader.

You may also find yourself copying someone else's actions or attitudes. This is good as long as you are following someone whose actions are pleasing to God. The apostle Paul told the believers at Corinth to follow him as he followed Jesus. He could say this to

167

the believers because he was striving to be like Jesus in everything he did. He was a good example for others to imitate. When you're imitating a leader who's following the Lord, it may help you become stronger in your Christian walk and be more like Jesus.

Of course, the best person to imitate is Jesus himself, but sometimes it helps to have an example you can physically see to follow. How do you know whether or not to copy someone? It's important that the person is openly following Jesus and that he or she acknowledges him as the leader. None of the person's decisions or actions should go against something the Bible teaches. But even the best Christian makes mistakes, so make sure your eyes are on Jesus as your true leader.

It's important to have your eyes on Jesus because God may choose you to be an example to someone. This person may be watching as you try to do the things Jesus wants you to do each day. Your good example may encourage him or her to follow the Lord too.

How can you know whether or not you should follow someone's example? How can you be a good example for someone else to imitate? List three ways you can be a good example for someone else.

85
Getting Wisdom

*The Lord grants wisdom! From his mouth
come knowledge and understanding.*

Proverbs 2:6

Solomon, the son of King David and Bathsheba,
was a godly man. One night God said to Solomon,
"What do you want? Ask, and I will give it to you!"
(2 Chronicles 1:7).

There were many things Solomon could have
asked for. He could have asked for a bigger kingdom,
more power, or endless riches. But he didn't. He said,
"O Lord God, please continue to keep your promise to
David my father, for you have made me king over a
people as numerous as the dust of the earth! Give me
the wisdom and knowledge to lead them properly, for
who could possibly govern this great people of yours?"
(2 Chronicles 1:9-10). Because God was pleased by
Solomon's request, he said he'd give Solomon not only
wisdom but also riches and fame.

Wisdom is more than just being smart. Memoriz-
ing facts and formulas doesn't make you wise. Wisdom
means knowing how to apply the lessons you learn
from past experiences, your knowledge, and your

good decision-making skills to your present circumstance. Solomon had a lot to say about wisdom in the book of Proverbs. For example, he said, "Joyful is the person who finds wisdom, the one who gains understanding. For wisdom is more profitable than silver, and her wages are better than gold" (Proverbs 3:13-14). Although Solomon had a lot of power and wealth, he believed that having wisdom was the best.

Solomon asked for wisdom in order to rule the people better. You can ask God for wisdom for your own life so you can know how to handle the situations you face. What should you do about the friend who is angry with you? How should you deal with a problem with your sister? What should you do about the teacher who doesn't seem to like you? How can you help a friend who is hurting? When you seek God's answers to these problems, you will gain wisdom. God's wisdom is the best kind. The Bible says, "The wisdom from above is first of all pure. It is also peace loving, gentle at all times, and willing to yield to others. It is full of mercy and the fruit of good deeds. It shows no favoritism and is always sincere" (James 3:17). Ask God to fill you with that kind of wisdom.

The book of Proverbs is filled with wisdom. Why not read through it? Read chapter one on the first day of the month. If you read one chapter a day, you can read through the whole book in a month.

86
Who Has the Corners?

*They couldn't bring him to Jesus because of
the crowd, so they dug a hole through the roof
above his head. Then they lowered the man
on his mat, right down in front of Jesus.*

MARK 2:4

Some men took their friend to see Jesus. The friend couldn't walk, and the men knew Jesus could heal him. But when they got to the house where Jesus was, it was so crowded that they couldn't get inside.

These friends didn't say, "Well, we tried," and then give up. They went onto the roof, cut a hole in it, and lowered the man through it. Jesus noticed them and healed the man. If the men hadn't believed Jesus could heal their friend, or if they had given up when they couldn't get him into the house, the man would not have been healed.

The paralyzed man had four friends to carry his mat when he needed help. It's important to have these kinds of friends in your life. You need people who are willing to grab the corners of your mat when you need assistance. Of course it may not be a real mat. You probably don't need that kind of help, but

you may need support with the difficult situations in your life.

People who want to be around you only when you're having fun aren't the kinds of friends who will grab a corner for you. Girls who want to be your friend only when you can do something for them in return aren't good corner holders either.

Your corner holders may be in your classroom, on your sports team, in your Sunday school class, or in your youth group. But they may not be. You might have an older sister who is the one who stands beside you when things get tough. Or it might be a teacher or a parent. Corner holders can be anyone who cares enough about you to be there for you.

Are you a corner holder for your friends? Can they come to you when they need to talk or need to know someone cares about their problems? Do you stand beside them when they are sad or down? Do you point them to an adult who can help when they have a problem that needs answers?

The paralyzed man had four friends willing to take him to Jesus to be healed. They didn't give up when helping got tough. Can you think of four people in your life who would do something like that for you? Thank God for them, and be sure to pray for them daily. Take an extra minute to thank them for being that kind of friend for you.

87
Part of the Body

*All of you together are Christ's body,
and each of you is a part of it.*
1 CORINTHIANS 12:27

God created your body in an amazing way. Each part of your body has a separate job, but all the parts work together to keep you going. You have eyes to see and ears to hear. You have feet to walk and hands to touch things. You have a brain to help you think and a heart to pump blood throughout your body.

There are some parts of your body you don't think about much, like your little toe or your pinky finger. But if you stub that toe on a chair, suddenly your whole body seems to hurt. Or when you get a splinter, suddenly you're very aware of your finger.

The Bible says that every believer is part of the body of Christ. As God's princess, you have a special part to play in God's work. It may seem as if some people are more important parts of the body. They are up front at church, singing, praying, or preaching. Other people seem more like little toes. You don't really notice them. They might be the people who count the offering after it's collected, make sure the bulletins are printed and ready to hand out each week, dust the pews, or set out the flower arrangements. Just like with the human body, some parts may not be as noticeable, but they are necessary to keep the body of Christ working as it should.

You have a special place in the body of Christ. You may be the one who hands out supplies in Sunday school or the one who cleans up afterward. You might be the friendly face who greets others at the door or sings in the children's or youth choir. You may be chosen to help a visitor feel welcome, or you might be selected to read the Scripture or sing when your church group visits the nursing home.

As part of the body of Christ, you have been given a special job to do by God. And it's one that you can do well, because he's chosen that job for you according to your abilities. So whether you feel like you play a big part or only a small one, remember that each part of the body is important. If you forget that, just remember how it feels to stub your toe. The whole body feels the pain because all the parts need to work together. The same is true in the body of Christ.

Think about all the things that have to be done to make your church run well. Who empties the trash? Who writes the bulletin? Who fills the Communion cups? Who washes the baptism robes? Be aware of the people who do the less noticeable jobs at your church, and thank them for what they do.

88

Clothing Fit for a Princess

*Don't be concerned about the outward beauty of fancy
hairstyles, expensive jewelry, or beautiful clothes.
You should clothe yourselves instead with the beauty
that comes from within, the unfading beauty of a
gentle and quiet spirit, which is so precious to God.*

I PETER 3:3-4

As God's princess, you can shine in this world. One way to shine is by dressing like a princess. You may have had a princess costume when you were young or dressed up as Cinderella, Belle, Snow White, or Aurora in a princess ball gown, complete with toy shoes and a tiara. That's one way to dress like a princess.

Another way to dress like a princess is to wear clothes that are not only attractive but also modest. Clothing that is modest doesn't show more of your body than is appropriate. Sometimes it's hard to find clothing that is both cute and appropriate, but with careful shopping, you and your mom can find clothes that are inexpensive, trendy, and modest.

The first thing to do is to discuss what modesty means to you and your mom. Should your shorts and skirts be no more than two inches above your knees?

Or will you use the rule that when you put your arms straight down, your shorts and skirts will at least touch your fingertips? Or will you pair cute leggings or tights with skirts for extra modesty and a stylish look?

Decide what types of shirts you'll wear too. Are spaghetti straps and tank tops okay, or will your shirts have sleeves? What about the neckline? This might not be something you worry about too much at your age, but it will become much more important as you enter your teen years. When it's hard to find modest necklines, layer shirts or put a high-cut tank top under a low-cut T-shirt.

Swimsuits can be a problem. Finding one that is both modest and stylish is challenging. You may end up ordering a swimsuit online to find one that is suitable for a princess.

The clothes you wear are a reflection of who you are. Ask a parent to help you find clothes that reflect your true beauty and allow you to look trendy while being modest.

Go through the clothes you already have. Do they pass the modesty test? If not, are there ways you can layer them or add tights or another accessory to make them more modest? If you aren't really into fashions and clothes yet, this might be a good time to look at what's available and start building your own look.

89
Families Are God's Idea

Father to the fatherless, defender of widows—this is God,
whose dwelling is holy. God places the lonely in families.
PSALM 68:5-6

The movie *Cheaper by the Dozen* is a comedy about a family with 12 children. Life is always crazy for this large family, but when the father moves the family to a new town despite their protests, things go from bad to worse. In the end all turns out well, of course, and the family has a closer bond than before.

This is only one movie about families. There are many other movies, as well as television shows and books, featuring families. These fictional families are all different, just like families in real life are different. Some families have a mom and dad, while others are run by a single parent or by grandparents. Some families have many children, and others have one child. Some children join a family by birth, others through adoption or foster care.

Even though there are many different family combinations, families are God's idea. Not only that, but he put you in the family he wanted you to be in. At times you may wonder why God chose the parents

and siblings he did for you, especially when you're in the middle of an argument with one of them or your mom interrupts your favorite show to ask you to fold clothes. God chose your family for you because he knew it was the right one for you.

Why did God put people in families? One reason is so that people would have a place where they are loved. Even if you don't always get along, your family members love you. No relationship is perfect, and sometimes relationships take a lot of work. Home is where you learn to do that work.

God also placed people in families to learn to work together to make things function well. Each person has responsibilities, and if one person neglects his or her responsibilities, things don't run as smoothly.

God also put people in families to serve and worship together. Your family may have a devotion time each day, or you may attend church together. You may have ways that you reach out in your community, too. If not, you might want to talk to a parent about that.

Families are God's idea, and he placed you in a family where you can learn the things you need to know for when you are an adult. When you get frustrated with other family members, ask God to give you the love and patience you need to thrive in your home.

What makes your family unique and special? Make a list of family members, and write down two things that are special about each one. Share that list with them.

90
Christmas Spirit
Year Round

[The angels said,] "Glory to God in highest heaven, and peace on earth to those with whom God is pleased."

LUKE 2:14

Imagine what it was like the night Jesus was born. Shepherds were out in the fields with their sheep. The night may have been dark and starless, or perhaps the shepherds were under a sky filled with stars. Everything was still, except for the occasional bleating of a sheep. Suddenly the sky was aglow with glorious light.

The shepherds were afraid, but an angel told them, "Don't be afraid! . . . I bring you good news that will bring great joy to all people. The Savior—yes, the Messiah, the Lord—has been born today in Bethlehem, the city of David! And you will recognize him by this sign: You will find a baby wrapped snugly in strips of cloth, lying in a manger" (Luke 2:10-12).

Then the sky was filled with angels saying, "Glory to God in highest heaven, and peace on earth to those with whom God is pleased." The shepherds hurried to find baby Jesus, and they worshiped him. Then they

179

went out and told everyone about what the angel had said.

Can you imagine how that one night changed the shepherds' lives? They could never forget the night they saw and heard the angels in the sky. Meeting the baby Jesus changed them forever.

Each year you celebrate Christmas, the birth of the Savior. Does the same sense of awe and wonder that filled the shepherds fill you as you think about Jesus coming to the earth as a baby? Or is Christmas more about parties, Christmas programs, gifts, or visits with relatives?

No matter what time of year it is, you can still cherish the Christmas story in your heart and have a sense of wonder about Jesus coming to the earth for you. You can be filled with awe, as the shepherds were, that the Son of God was born in a lowly stable in order to live among humanity.

Celebrate Christmas in your heart year-round, and let that sense of wonder spread to those around you, especially those who don't yet have the hope of Jesus in their lives.

No matter what time of year it is, take time to read the Christmas story from Luke 2. Thank God for the gift of his Son, and share the message of salvation with someone today.

91
The Hundred Acre Wood

Be patient with each other, making allowance
for each other's faults because of your love.
EPHESIANS 4:2

When you were younger, you may have enjoyed the Winnie the Pooh stories set in the Hundred Acre Wood. The stories are about the adventures of Pooh, Tigger, Eeyore, and Rabbit, four very different characters whose differences sometimes cause disagreements but also help to solve problems.

Pooh is a somewhat lazy bear who loves everyone. Pooh is easy to love, too, because he's accepting and rarely complains. In fact, sometimes the others have to try to figure out what's bothering Pooh, because he doesn't freely express his feelings. He's also careful not to hurt other people's feelings, and he is a peacemaker.

Tigger, on the other hand, is a bouncing bundle of energy who's the life of the party. He likes to be around people, and it doesn't matter what they are doing as long as it's fun. He is impulsive, and sometimes it's hard to get him focused on what needs to be done.

Eeyore wanders around the Hundred Acre Wood filled with gloom. When a problem arises, he is a

181

careful thinker who notices the little details others miss. He sees the obstacles others may overlook.

Rabbit is someone who knows what needs to be accomplished and does it. Sometimes he doesn't consider others' feelings when he has a goal he wants to reach. While Eeyore is planning and Tigger is out having fun, Rabbit is getting the job done.

Sometimes the characters' differences cause problems. Rabbit hurts people's feelings. Tigger's high energy annoys gloomy Eeyore, and Pooh can come across as lazy. But at the same time, their strengths balance each other. Eeyore tells others what to look out for. Rabbit works to reach a goal. Pooh loves everyone and encourages them. Tigger adds the fun and enthusiasm.

Are you like Pooh, Tigger, Eeyore, or Rabbit? What about your friends and family? Just as in the Hundred Acre Wood, differences among you may be annoying at times. But your strengths balance each other. And that's what makes life fun and interesting.

Even if your friends or family members are different from you, be patient with them. God asks us to love others and be patient with their faults, whether they are Poohs, Tiggers, Eeyores, or Rabbits.

Watch a Winnie the Pooh movie with your family. Which character does each family member resemble? How do those differences cause arguments between you and your family members? What strengths do each of you have to help the others?

92
Envy

I observed that most people are motivated to success because they envy their neighbors. But this, too, is meaningless.

<small>ECCLESIASTES 4:4</small>

Have you ever wished that you had someone else's ability to sing? Have you ever hoped your parents would buy you a cool phone like the one your friend has? Have you ever wanted to go on an exciting vacation like the one your friend is going on? It's pretty normal to want more talent or cool things, but when desiring them makes you discontent with what you already have, you are probably feeling envy.

Solomon, the wisest man who ever lived, said that envy is meaningless. If envy is meaningless, it's a good thing to get rid of. How can you do that? By being thankful for the talents and possessions you have. That answer may sound simple, but it's true. There will always be someone else who has more talent and stuff than you do, but there are also many people who have less than you do.

There are people who lack even the basic necessities of food, clothing, and clean water. All you have

to do is read about the problems in developing countries to realize this. While you are complaining that your computer runs too slowly or you have only a pay-per-minute cell phone, people in other parts of the world are dying because their water supply is unsafe or because a storm destroyed their crops.

And if it seems as if others always have more talent than you, focus on your strengths. Maybe you will never sing a solo, get the lead in a play, or make the winning basket in a championship game, but look for what you can do. Can you cook or bake? Are you good with younger children or the elderly? Can you draw portraits or write poetry? Solve difficult math problems? Look for the things you are good at, and work to improve them. Look for ways to use your talents to make someone else's life a little brighter or a little better.

Envy will make you unhappy and discontent with what you have. The cure for envy is to look at all you do have and all you can do and to be thankful for the things God has given you. Ask God to help you do that this week.

Take time to make a list today. Set a timer for three minutes, and write down as many things as you can think of that you are thankful for. If your list isn't very long, it might be time to stop and think about all you really have.

93
Making a Difference

Trust in the LORD and do good. Then you
will live safely in the land and prosper.

PSALM 37:3

Have you ever done something just because a friend did it? Have you ever asked your mom to buy you a certain piece of clothing because everyone else at school seemed to be wearing it? Have you watched a certain television show because everyone was talking about it and you felt left out? If you've done any of these things, you've been affected by peer pressure.

Remember how we talked about not doing wrong things just because others were doing them (see p. 123 for a reminder)? We saw that a princess needs to stand out for God. But peer pressure isn't always wrong. Sometimes it's a good thing. If you did a good deed because someone else did, that's great. If you are kind and encouraging toward someone because you saw a friend acting that way, that's good too. Or if you decided to dress modestly or to listen to only good music because someone you admire does, that's another example of positive peer pressure.

As God's princess, you can be the one to set the

example and encourage others to do the same. That's using positive peer pressure. How can you do this? Start each day by asking God to help you make good choices and to do the things he wants you to do. Then follow God's leading and encourage others to join you. Be the first to welcome a new girl at school or church. Be the one who sits with a lonely student at lunch. Set the example in studying and working hard at school-work. Volunteer for the less desirable jobs, like wiping the lunch tables or cleaning up after an activity.

If you take the lead in choosing to do right and do it with a good attitude and a smile, others will want to join you. You will shine as God's princess.

Can you think of times when you followed positive peer pressure—you did something good because someone you admired was doing it? Think of three ways you can be the one to do good things that others will want to copy.

94
A Journey with God

*Rebekah and her servant girls mounted the
camels and followed the man. So Abraham's
servant took Rebekah and went on his way.*

GENESIS 24:61

Abraham wanted to find a wife for his son Isaac.
Abraham sent a servant, Eliezer, to his homeland to choose a wife. Eliezer realized this was a very
important decision, so he said to God, "See, I am standing here beside this spring, and the young women of
the town are coming out to draw water. This is my
request. I will ask one of them, 'Please give me a drink
from your jug.' If she says, 'Yes, have a drink, and I
will water your camels, too!'—let her be the one you
have selected as Isaac's wife. This is how I will know
that you have shown unfailing love to my master"
(Genesis 24:13-14).

Rebekah came to the well to draw water. When
Eliezer asked her for water, she offered not only to get
him water but also to get water for his camels. That's
how Eliezer knew Rebekah was the right wife for Isaac.
He went to talk to her family.

Can you imagine someone showing up at your

door and telling your parents that he wanted you as a wife for a man you'd never met? Not only that, but you'd have to leave your home and travel with him on a long journey in order to marry the man. That's what happened with Rebekah. Of course, things like that were more common in Bible times, but Rebekah had to be willing to accept the fact that leaving her family was part of God's plan for her and then travel by camel to Isaac's home. Rebekah went with Eliezer, married Isaac, and gave birth to twin sons, Jacob and Esau. In making the journey, she fulfilled God's plan for her and played an important role in Jewish history.

God has a journey for you, too. It may not be a trip to a new land like Rebekah's was, but your journey means going wherever God leads you. For now, God may be leading you to school, to your neighborhood, and to your church, or maybe even to go on a summer mission trip with your youth group. Later the journey may lead you to college, a job, marriage, or mother-hood. Like Rebekah, you can follow the course God has planned for you and know that God will lead you to the places where he wants to use you.

Read the story of Rebekah's journey from Genesis 24. What things stand out to you about Rebekah? How are you like her, or how do you wish you were like her?

95
Leading the Way

"Very well," [Deborah] replied, "I will go with you.
But you will receive no honor in this venture, for the
LORD's victory over Sisera will be at the hands of a
woman." So Deborah went with Barak to Kedesh.

JUDGES 4:9

If someone asked you to name a famous woman leader, who would you name? Would it be Joan of Arc, the peasant girl who helped lead the French in battle against England? Or maybe it would be Margaret Thatcher, the former British prime minister who wasn't afraid to speak her mind. How about Deborah, one of God's princesses in Old Testament times?

Deborah lived during the time of the judges. She would sit under a tree, and people would come to her for advice because they knew that she listened to God and was wise.

One day Deborah called for Barak, a military leader, and told him to take 10,000 men and fight against Sisera, the captain of an enemy army. Barak said he would go, but only if Deborah went into battle with him. A woman in battle was very uncommon in Bible times. Deborah agreed to go with Barak, but she

told him he wouldn't get the credit for the victory. So Deborah, along with Barak, assembled the troops and then went into battle.

Barak was not willing to lead the men into battle without Deborah, but she was ready to go into battle knowing that God was the one who would provide the victory. Deborah was strong in spirit, faith, and body, and that made her a good leader for the people. She saw what needed to be done and did it.

Are you a princess who takes charge and does what needs to be done? Are you willing to lead the way if God asks you to? You won't lead your friends into battle, but you might lead them in a community service activity, a mission project, or another opportunity to do good. You might lead the way in getting a rule changed or added, or in starting a mentoring program for younger students at your school. If you are homeschooled, you might be the one to suggest and plan a field trip for your local homeschool group or find a way for them to be involved in the community.

Ask God to show you if he wants you to lead the way in accomplishing something for him. If he does, he'll be with you each step of the way. Be sure to have trusted adults and good friends for support, too. Like Deborah, you can be known as someone who bravely steps out in faith.

Are there areas where God might use you to lead the way? Talk to an adult about how you can do that.

96
Being Loyal

Ruth replied, "Don't ask me to leave you and turn back. Wherever you go, I will go; wherever you live, I will live. Your people will be my people, and your God will be my God."

RUTH 1:16

One time there was a famine in Bethlehem. A Jewish man named Elimelech moved to Moab with his wife, Naomi, and their two sons so they would have food. Elimelech was Jewish and worshiped God, but Moab was a pagan country, one where the people worshiped idols. While the family was living in this foreign country, the two sons married Moabite women. One of the women was named Ruth.

Things didn't go well for Elimelech's family in Moab. Elimelech died. Later, both of his sons died. Naomi and her two daughters-in-law were left alone with no husbands to care for them. Naomi decided it was time to go back to Bethlehem, where she still had family and friends. One of her daughters-in-law, Orpah, returned to her family. But the other daughter-in-law, Ruth, decided to go with Naomi to Bethlehem.

Naomi tried to persuade Ruth to stay in Moab,

but Ruth stayed with her mother-in-law even though Naomi was a bitter woman because of all she had lost. Ruth chose to give up her pagan ways and worship the true God. She became one of God's princesses.

When they reached Bethlehem, Ruth didn't feel sorry for herself because she was in a strange country. She didn't ask for pity because her husband had died. She didn't let her grief keep her from doing what needed to be done. She went to work to care for herself and Naomi.

In those times, when farmers harvested their fields, they'd leave behind the grain that was dropped. The poor could come and gather that grain to feed themselves. That's how Ruth provided for herself and Naomi.

Ruth gathered grain in a field that belonged to a man named Boaz. After she married Boaz, she took care of Naomi. God blessed Ruth and allowed her to be a part of Jesus' family tree by being the great-grandmother of King David.

God wants you to be loyal to your family and to take care of your family members. When you choose to spend time playing or working with them, you are honoring God, who gave you your family.

Look for opportunities to put your family members first this week. Take time to play a game with a younger sibling, or allow an older sibling to choose which movie to watch, even if it's your turn to pick. Do a job for a family member, and help without being asked.

97
God Answers Prayers

[Hannah] made this vow: "O LORD of Heaven's Armies, if you will look upon my sorrow and answer my prayer and give me a son, then I will give him back to you. He will be yours for his entire lifetime, and as a sign that he has been dedicated to the LORD, his hair will never be cut."

1 SAMUEL 1:11

Hannah was a princess of God with a heavy heart. She longed to have a baby, but it hadn't happened yet. To make matters worse, her husband had another wife, which was common in those times, and that wife had children. She made fun of Hannah for not being able to have a child.

Each year Hannah traveled with her husband and the other wife to the Tabernacle at Shiloh. Hannah was sad that she didn't have children, so she went into the Tabernacle to plead with God for a son. Eli, the priest, saw Hannah's lips moving but didn't hear any words coming out, so he thought she was drunk. Hannah explained to him that she was pouring out her heart to God. Eli told her to go in peace, because God would answer her prayer.

Hannah did give birth to a son, and she dedicated

him to the Lord's work. When he was old enough, she took him to live at the Tabernacle and serve God there.

Hannah desired a child, and she told God about it and pleaded with him for what she wanted. Because Hannah loved the Lord and desired to serve him, God answered her prayer.

God asks you to tell him about your desires, and he wants to answer them. He will answer your prayers if the things you desire are things that are part of God's plan for you. Hannah didn't pray for children in order to compete with the other wife or for her own selfish reason. She prayed for a son to dedicate back to God. And God honored that request.

If your heart is in tune with God, and you desire his will for your life, chances are your requests will be ones that he wants to answer. When you pray, ask God to take away any wrong desires and show you what he wants for you. Pray often for those things, and watch God work in your life.

Take time to read about Hannah in 1 Samuel 1. You can read about her son, Samuel, in the rest of 1 Samuel. Become a woman of prayer like Hannah by asking God to lead you and to provide the things you need to serve him better.

98

In the Right Place at the Right Time

[Mordecai said,] "If you keep quiet at a time like this, deliverance and relief for the Jews will arise from some other place, but you and your relatives will die. Who knows if perhaps you were made queen for just such a time as this?"

ESTHER 4:14

Esther was God's princess whom God placed in the right place at the right time to deliver his people. Esther was a Jew living in Babylonia, which was under Persian rule. There were many Jews in the land because the Jewish people had been taken captive and brought there long before. When they were released, many chose to stay because they had homes and families in Babylonia. They didn't want to make the long trip back to their homeland.

There was a man named Haman who was a powerful official in the Persian kingdom. He thought all the people should bow to him when he went by, but Mordecai, Esther's cousin, wouldn't bow before him. Haman knew Mordecai was a Jew and made a plan to get rid of

him and all the other Jews. Haman didn't realize Esther was also a Jew and a relative of Mordecai's.

Mordecai found out about Haman's plan and asked Esther to talk to the king, her husband, about it. Esther was nervous about approaching the king, who didn't know she was a Jew, but Mordecai told her that God might have put her in the palace for the very reason of saving the Jews. Esther realized he was right, so she told the king about Haman's plan and revealed that she, too, was a Jew.

The king had Haman killed, and the Jews were allowed to defend themselves against those trying to destroy them and were victorious in that effort.

God put Esther in a certain place to accomplish something. Esther didn't know ahead of time that was why she was there, so some of the things that happened to her may not have made sense at the time. But it was all part of God's plan.

You don't know all that God wants you to accomplish for him, but be aware that he may allow certain things to happen in your life to get you where he needs you to be. As you go through the day, remind yourself that God has you where you are "for just such a time as this."

Esther made a big difference for the Jewish people because she was willing to be used where she was. Take time to read through the book of Esther, and allow God to speak to you through her story.

99

Are You a Mary or a Martha?

*[Jesus and the disciples] came to a certain village
where a woman named Martha welcomed
him into her home. Her sister, Mary, sat at the
Lord's feet, listening to what he taught.*

LUKE 10:38-39

Two sisters, Mary and Martha, were God's princesses in the New Testament. In fact, they were friends of Jesus along with their brother, Lazarus. When Jesus was in Bethany, he'd stop by and visit with them.

The sisters were very different from each other. When Jesus was going to visit them, Martha saw what needed to be done, organized it, and completed the job. But Mary would focus on Jesus, sitting near him and listening to him. This upset Martha. She felt she was doing all the work while Mary just sat around. Martha even complained to Jesus about it, saying, "Lord, doesn't it seem unfair to you that my sister just sits here while I do all the work? Tell her to come and help me" (Luke 10:40).

If Martha expected Jesus to tell Mary to get busy

helping, she was disappointed. Jesus said, "My dear Martha, you are worried and upset over all these details! There is only one thing worth being concerned about. Mary has discovered it, and it will not be taken away from her" (Luke 10:41-42). Jesus wasn't saying it was wrong to want to clean the house and cook for him, but he was telling Martha that wasn't what really mattered. The important thing was spending time with him.

God needs princesses who know how to both worship and serve but who remember that the worshiping is the more important of the two. You can worship at church by being involved in the singing, praying, and Bible teaching. Worship isn't just about music. It's an attitude of the heart. You worship God by putting the focus on him and getting closer to him. Your service is a result of that relationship. It's not a separate thing. Because of your love for God, you want to do things to serve him and others. Both worshiping and serving are important, but the more important one is worshiping.

What are some ways you worship? What can you do to make your worship more meaningful? In what areas do you serve God? What are some new ways you can serve God? If you aren't sure of the answers to these questions, ask God to show you what he wants you to do. Talk to a parent or Sunday school teacher, and share your desire to worship and serve. He or she may have some suggestions for you.

100

Saying Yes to God

Mary responded, "I am the Lord's servant.
May everything you have said about me
come true." And then the angel left her.

Luke 1:38

Mary, the mother of Jesus, was one of God's princesses chosen for a very special job. Mary was a common Jewish girl. But because she loved the Lord, she was chosen for the greatest privilege of all— being the earthly mother of the Son of God.

In our society, it's often the smartest, wealthiest, most talented, and most beautiful people who get chosen for the highest honors, but that's not how God chooses. In fact, he told Samuel this when it was time to choose a king: "The LORD said to Samuel, 'Don't judge by his appearance or height, for I have reject- ed him. The LORD doesn't see things the way you see them. People judge by outward appearance, but the LORD looks at the heart'" (1 Samuel 16:7). God had chosen David, a young shepherd boy who did not look like royalty, to be king. In the same way, God looked at Mary's heart when he chose her to be the mother of the Savior.

What does God look for in the heart? Love for him and love for others. Obedience to him and his Word and a willingness to do what he asks without questioning. Of course, he knows his princesses aren't perfect, so he understands that sometimes your faith wavers, you question him, or you fail to be obedient. He knows your motives and desires, and those are what really count.

If you want to be used by God, start by doing the things you already know he wants you to do. Obey your parents and teachers. Put others ahead of yourself. Spend time reading the Bible and praying. Attend church, and really listen to what's being said.

God speaks to you through nudges to your heart, so if you get a feeling that there's something you're supposed to do, that may be God prompting you to action. If you feel guilty ignoring it, the Holy Spirit is urging you to obey.

Want to do big things for the Lord? Focus on following God and listening for his directions for you. Then be like Mary, and say yes to God.

Do you ever feel God prompting you to do something? Do you say yes even when it seems hard? Read about how Mary said yes to God in Luke 1:26-56. This section of Scripture also includes the special song Mary sang when she found out that she would be the mother of Jesus.

Now What?

Now that you've finished this book, think back over all the things you've learned about being one of God's princesses. What things seem most important to you? What changes have you made or will you make because you are God's princess? Remember to always listen to your heavenly King and follow him. Then live the adventure he has for you, one day at a time.

Acknowledgments

A special thanks to
Rick: best friend for life
Tyler: firstborn
Jessica: firstborn princess
Jeff: my first Haitian sensation
Adam: compassionate warrior
Jasmine: my joy and song
Kaleb and Kayla: chosen ones
For all their support and willingness
to help out while I wrote.

The Tyndale team who saw the possibilities
in this book and brought it to life:
Katara Patton, Erin Gwynne, and Susan Taylor

Teresa Cleary for her suggestions and input

Also by Katrina Cassel

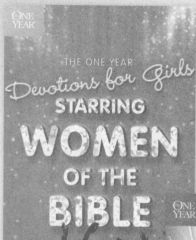

The One Year® Devotions for Girls Starring Women of the Bible

The One Year® Book of Bible Trivia for Kids

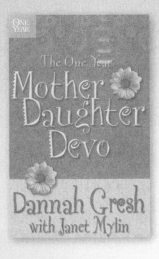
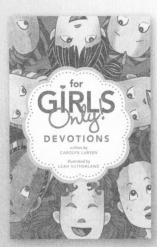

About the Author

Katrina (Kathy) Cassel is the author of several Tyndale books, including *The One Year Devotions for Girls Starring Women of the Bible* and *The One Year Book of Bible Trivia*. She's also the author of *The Christian Girl's Guide to Being Your Best*, *The Christian Girl's Guide to the Bible*, and several other books for the teen/tween audience. Katrina has a BS in elementary education from Grace College, Winona Lake, Indiana, and an MEd with a reading specialty from the University of North Dakota. She has worked with children of all ages in a variety of educational and church settings. She and her husband have eight children and live in Panama City, Florida.